See Yourself in the Bible

See Yourself in the Bible

WALTER RUSSELL BOWIE

HARPER & ROW, PUBLISHERS
New York, Evanston, and London

ACKNOWLEDGMENTS

Grateful acknowledgment is made to the following who have granted permission for the reprinting of copyrighted material from the books listed below:

DOUBLEDAY & COMPANY, INC. for extracts from *The Sons of Martha,* copyright 1907 by Rudyard Kipling, from RUDYARD KIPLING'S VERSE: DEFINITIVE EDITION. Reprinted by permission of Mrs. George Bambridge and Doubleday & Company, Inc.

DOUBLEDAY & COMPANY, INC. for extracts from *Tomlinson* from "Barrack Room Ballads" by Rudyard Kipling, from RUDYARD KIPLING'S VERSE: DEFINITIVE EDITION. Reprinted by permission of Doubleday & Company, Inc., and Mrs. George Bambridge, Messrs. Macmillan & Company, Ltd. and the Macmillan Company of Canada.

SOCIETY OF AUTHORS for extract from *Saint Joan* by George Bernard Shaw, copyright 1924.

FIRST EDITION

LIBRARY OF CONGRESS CATALOG CARD NUMBER: 67-11500

To
DOTTIE
Who Is in This Book

As in the case of *Men of Fire* and *Women of Light,* my special thanks to Miss Lisa McGaw for careful scrutiny of the manuscript and verification of details.

W.R.B.

Contents

Introduction

SOME YEARS ago I wrote a book called *Great Men of the Bible,* and lately it occurred to me to try to write a second one, called *More Great Men of the Bible.* But then the realization came that it is not only, and perhaps not chiefly, the people who were great who make the Bible come closest home to us. The Bible includes the whole range of human beings such as we know in our place and time: the good and the bad and the in-between; some who did their best, and some who did nothing or made a botch of what little they began to do, and some—like most of us—whose record would be a mixed-up matter. It is a mirror wide enough to reflect all life. That is the reason, then, for the title of this book, and especially for the second word in it: *See Yourself in the Bible.*

But there is something in the Bible which gives it a different dimension from ordinary histories. It tells about people, but above all it tells about God and about people in relationship to God. Most of us would like to know much more about that relationship than we do. We recognize that unless we are taken hold of by something bigger than ourselves life can be flat and shallow. But how does it come about—this difference between a life that has meaning and a life that has none? Somebody may tell us in general terms what the answer is, but we may fail to grasp it unless we *see* it. To look at men and women of the Bible, in their vividness and their variety, may help us see it. In face of the failures of some of them, we may find ourselves saying, "That is exactly the way I might fail"; and in the light of what the grace of God wrought in others of them—and even in ordinary ones—we may say, "I begin to understand where the power is that can make *me* what I ought to be."

WALTER RUSSELL BOWIE

Alexandria, Virginia
July 1, 1966

See Yourself in the Bible

1.

Knowing What Matters Most

. . . Esau, who sold his birthright for
a single meal.
HEBREWS 12:16

THINGS DO not always turn out the way we expect, especially about
people. Someone who we would have thought must surely go a long way
falls short, and someone else who did not seem at first to amount to
much outstrips him. The reason for failure may not be that a man
has done anything deliberately bad. It may be just that he has never
taken the trouble to consider what is best, and then to shape his
choices in the light of it.

In the Book of Genesis there is the story of two brothers whose
names have been long familiar, Jacob and Esau. That is the order in
which they are usually spoken of: Jacob first, as though he were the
more important. He did become more important, but one would not
have expected that at the beginning. The two were twins, but Esau
was the elder twin. Also as they began to grow up, he was much the
more attractive. Their mother might be partial to Jacob, but Esau
was his father's favorite. And seemingly with reason. Jacob was the
stay-at-home, sit-by-the-fire sort, but Esau was the boy and man who
loved the out-of-doors: vigorous, warmblooded and warmhearted too.

Isaac, his father, was an old man and growing feeble. He could not
go where he wanted to go or do much of what he might have wished
to do, but he knew he could depend on Esau. One day when he had
a desire for something special to eat that might strengthen him, he
asked Esau to go out and shoot a deer and bring him venison. So
Esau went out to hunt. He did find a deer and shot it with his arrow,
and laying the deer across his broad shoulders he brought it home.
Evidently it had been a long day, and now at the end of it he was
hungry. The one thing he wanted was a good hot supper. And when

he got near home, the first thing he was aware of was the welcome smell of something very savory that Jacob was cooking.

"Let me have some of that!" said Esau.

Well, Jacob would—but at a price, for he had a crafty purpose. He knew how impulsive Esau was, so bent on getting what he wanted when he wanted it that he would not stop to think what he might be risking. "What about a little bargain?" Jacob suggested. "You were born to the birthright, Esau, but what good is that to a hungry man. You have the birthright, but I have the supper. You promise me the birthright, and then come and eat all you want."

The birthright was the spiritual privilege which belonged to the eldest son. It meant that he would succeed his father as the family's head. He would be the family representative, not only to men but also to God. Esau knew all that, but he did not stop to think about it. Perhaps he supposed that Jacob was only teasing. But anyhow, he was not going to concern himself about anything so unsubstantial as a birthright now. His hungry body was talking louder than his mind and spirit. "Supper first; and bother about the birthright another time. If Jacob wants the birthright so much, let him have it."

The vivid story in the Book of Genesis goes on to tell how Jacob did get the birthright, to Esau's bitter distress when he found that he had really lost it. While he was out hunting, Rebekah, who was mother of them both but who favored Jacob, had dressed Jacob up to seem like Esau, had shown him how to prepare meat like the venison which Esau had gone out to get, and then had taken Jacob in where blind old Issac could lay his hands on him while Jacob told him that he was Esau. So Isaac, deceived, had given to Jacob the blessing which belonged to Esau; and once bestowed, it could not be taken back.

On the basis of the story as it has unfolded thus far, the impulse of everyone would be to like Esau and to dislike Jacob—and, actually, "dislike" might seem altogether too mild a word. But the strange fact is that of the two brothers it was Jacob and not Esau who became the more significant. How that could be we shall consider later, but our first interest is in Esau; both in regard to his strength and in regard to his calamitous limitation.

I

The immediate attractiveness of Esau is easy to understand. He had the charm which can always belong to the physically vigorous man. That charm is represented in the popular athlete. A boy in school or college stands out above the crowd: on the running track, in the crew, on the baseball diamond, or—most glamorously—on the football field. He becomes for a time the hero. Not only his own generation but older men also who flock to see him have admiration for him, as Isaac had for the virile Esau when he went out to hunt. And that is good. A strong body is a gift from God which a man may rightly rejoice in, and use to the full development of its energies. The man who does have physical prowess and adds this to his other endowments is to that degree so much the more commanding person.

Theodore Roosevelt owed part of the immense fascination he had for many people and the influence he exerted over them to the vigor of his body, which seemed to radiate force like a charged dynamo. And what he had he gained the hard way. Originally of a delicate constitution, prone to sicknesses, he deliberately set himself to overcome his handicaps; taking himself away from soft surroundings, out to what was still the frontier, among cowboys and ranch-hands and big-game hunters, facing the tough demands of hard work and physical risk. So also in the gallant figure of John Fitzgerald Kennedy one felt a power which could never have come from physical flabbiness: the power of a disciplined endurance which made him able in the Second World War, when the ship he commanded had been sunk in the South Pacific, to rescue a wounded member of his crew by dragging the man behind him by a strap held in his teeth, as he swam four miles to an island which was their single hope. No one remembering that can fail to know that there is something magnificent in a body trained and fit.

But suppose physical strength is the only kind of strength a person has, and suppose the exploitation of it makes everything else seem to him unimportant. For instance, the boy of exceptional promise is persuaded to come to a school or a college by the bait of an "athletic scholarship"—the smooth term that hides the financial bribery by which much so-called amateur athletics may be turned into a racket for the benefit of hired coaches backed up by loud alumni who have not outgrown their adolescence. Then the boy who had in him so much that was attractive may have all his sense of values twisted. He had a birthright which was something bigger than the bare fact of beating others at a game, the birthright of developing his full self. But that larger possibility gets lost in the lesser one. He feeds on applause, as Esau fed on Jacob's cooking and was hungry for it. Then there may be observed the unhappy result, not always but too often true, that the boy and man whose name was on everybody's lips in school and college, ten years later is forgotten, because he had been more involved with his body than with his mind. In reaching out for the exciting quick satisfaction he has let slip the better part of what he ought to have been in college for; and so like Esau, he may have "sold his birthright for a single meal."

But what we have thought and said thus far is not an adequate representation of the kind of man who is like Esau—not adequate in regard to his original attractiveness nor in regard to the poignancy of what was lost in him. As we remembered before, Esau had not only a strong body; he had also a warm heart. His emotions could be quick and passionate, but they could be easy going too. He did not like to keep himself keyed up. When he first realized that Jacob had tricked him out of the birthright and of his father's blessing, he was furious, and Jacob had to get away quickly to avoid his wrath. But when Jacob came back years later from exile, and with a guilty apprehension tried to conciliate Esau by all sorts of gifts and soft messages sent ahead, the tolerant generosity of Esau's spirit became more conspicuous in contrast to those little contrived devices. He did not want any placating gifts from Jacob. He was not that sort of man. Jacob could come back now if he wanted to. What had happened did not matter so much that it could not be brushed aside. After all, was he particularly the worse off for having lost the birthright?

Did *anything* matter too much? The fact that Esau could wonder whether it did was part of his charm, and also part of his fateful weakness. If he had been more deeply concerned with what the birthright meant, he could not have yielded to the momentary urging that let him bargain it away. And that same failure may be repeated in men of every generation who have the instinctive value judgments which Esau had.

Consider, for example, the field of public affairs and politics. Municipalities have been corrupted because there are people who act on the idea that some immediate advantage they can get is worth more than holding to high principle. The ward leaders of a political organization want to build up the organization's power, and how will they do it? By remembering that the characteristics which were in Esau may crop up everywhere in human nature. Like Esau, the people at large may want some special thing so much and want it so instantly that they do not stop to think of the price they may have to pay for getting it. Here is a family that is short of food, so the ward leader sends them a basket full of groceries. Here are some others who have no fuel, so he sends them a bag of coal. He does not say out loud, as Jacob said to Esau, "Will you give me your birthright in return?" But that is actually what he is beginning to devise; to get the people obligated, so that when the next election comes they will vote the way he tells them, keep his political machine in office and let him therefore share the big benefits which political influence can command; and never mind the little fact that they have thus sold out to him the birthright of their responsible citizenship.

In the *Carolina Israelite,* Harry Golden has written of "How Tammany Did It" when he was growing up in New York City.

Big Tim Sullivan was the Tammany Hall power on the Bowery of New York. . . . He made a fortune out of his position as a Tammany district leader—principally from "concessions" to gambling houses and "Raines Law" hotels. . . . Big Tim gave us East Side kids a trip up the Hudson every year. A trip to Bear Mountain; and the name "Big Tim" was blessed in thousands of households.

Big Tim made a speech to his constituents. "The reformers think just because I have a little money, there must be something wrong. I say, 'To hell with reform.' " The crowd cheered. "And," continued Sullivan, "if I have done wrong, I have always thought I have done right, and I was always good to the poor." The women in the crowd wept openly, and most of the men were dabbing their wet cheeks with handkerchiefs.[1]

The "Big Tim" in any city may seem so thoroughly likable that he wins the heart of the crowd; big, genial, capable of generous emotions —as also Esau was. He does not like to think that his methods are doing anybody harm. But the fact is that in the whole situation, what with the readiness of the people to take the bait of temporary material benefits and with the feeling of the politician that matters of principle do not need to be concerned with overmuch, a whole community may lose its conscience. That happens when one person or another, in everyday considerations and choices, begins to think and say,

> Ah, take the Cash, and let the Credit go
> Nor heed the rumble of a distant Drum![2]

Can any one of us fail to recognize the possible relevance of all this to himself, in ways still more personal and familiar? Who is there that may not be inclined, as Esau was, to seize some immediate satisfaction at the cost of a long-range good, and imagine meanwhile that the consequences will not matter much. The cash of the easy self-pleasing is alluring, and the rumble of the drum of retribution

[1] Harry Golden, *Only in America* (New York: Pocket Books—Permabook, 1959), p. 196.
[2] *The Rubáiyát of Omar Kháyyám,* trans. by Edward Fitzgerald.

seems so remote that the ears can be stopped against it. A boy is born into a family of fine traditions. He can inherit not only respectability but distinction too. Instead of that, he may treat his inheritance not as a privilege to be lived up to, but as a bothersome restraint to be got rid of. Like the wayward boy in Jesus' parable of "the prodigal son" he may want to break the home ties completely, and go off on his own headstrong course. Suppose, however, that—as may be more likely—he is not inclined to that sort of extreme rebellion. He will not betake himself to some "far country" or indulge in "riotous living." But he may register a failure hardly less sad, though it is not so conspicuous. He does not despise his birthright; he only ignores it. He does nothing evil, but neither does he do anything much worthwhile. He is too ready—as Esau was when he smelled Jacob's cooking—to feel that when anything agreeable is at hand he must certainly have it. Those who know him and like him for his general attractiveness nevertheless regard him with a growing disappointment. They may say of him, "He has too great a birthright to be so casual and easygoing. His family has been linked with great causes in this community. He could give more of himself, as others did, to generous public service—but he will not if it takes too much effort, or if he has to postpone some obvious satisfaction which is close at hand. He has an amiable inclination to live up to what is expected of him, but you cannot depend upon him when the going gets hard. If carrying on requires too much sacrifice of immediate advantage, if loyalty to the long purpose looks impractical, he may say, as Esau did to Jacob, 'What profit is the birthright to me now?' "

In George Eliot's *Romola,* there is an unforgettable phrase which sums up the fateful process by which a man of high possibilities may let his strength be traded off: "He tried to slip away from everything that was unpleasant." *He* did—and what about you and me?

II

Alongside the figure of Esau in the graphic Old Testament description there is the figure of Jacob, his brother. As compared with Esau he seems at first to be the far less commendable person of the two, and in original appearance he certainly was. Whoever came face to face with the two of them would have said at the outset that anyone in his senses would prefer to have Esau for a friend, not Jacob; and if any large destiny would be fulfilled in either of them, it would be in Esau. With his genial, devil-may-care ways, he just *looked* like a man whom everybody had to like.

But the ultimate facts of life and character lie deeper than what superficial observation sees. In Jacob there would be revealed qualities which Esau lacked, and without which no man—no matter how fascinating may be his manner—can gain the strength to make the most of life and let life make the most of him.

First is the realization that the things the physical senses reach out for are not the things that are most important. Every human being who has attained any sort of mental and moral development knows that theoretically, but *realizing* it is a different matter. There was the crucial moment when Esau did not realize it. To get what smelled good and tasted good, to satisfy his appetite, pushed other considerations out of his mind. He would get what he had wanted when he wanted it, and to curb that impulse of his would take self-control which he did not choose to bother with. But Jacob, inferior to Esau in many ways though he was, had begun to subject his body to his mind. He might naturally have preferred to eat his own supper instead of giving it to Esau. But he had a purpose in his mind that was more important than his appetite: a mixed sort of purpose, but one which at least was a step above the urging of the flesh.

The second thing about Jacob was an awareness of God which took his mixed motives and began to lift them not only above the flesh but above the meaner elements in his mind. He wanted the birthright which belonged to Esau. One reason why he wanted it was for the prestige he personally would get from it—a reason that was crude and common. But there was something else also. He had at least a dawning sense of the spiritual meaning of the birthright, as a sort of priesthood which would make him responsible for bringing himself and the whole family more reverently into relationship with God. That was why this man with all his faults could have the experience which is described in the twenty-eighth chapter of the Book of Genesis. At one of the darkest moments of his life, when he was fleeing from the wrath of Esau, he lay down at night in a bleak wilderness, with only a stone on which to rest his head. Yet there he had a dream, and in his dream he saw "a ladder set up on the earth, and the top of it reached to heaven; and behold, the angels of God were ascending and descending on it!"

A strange, unlikely dream, we might think, to have come to Jacob! By what accident would *he* have a vision of a ladder reaching up toward heaven? Yet it was not an accident. Dreams do not come by some unrelated chance, but out of something that may have been quite hidden in the mind and heart of the one who dreams, but which hidden or not was *there*. That vision of the ladder was an expression of what Jacob in some subconscious way at least was reaching for. His life had moved on a low level, but there was a higher one that he began to want. When he coveted the birthright, it was not only for what worldly advantage might be in it. He had a glimmering of a spiritual dedication which the birthright was meant to symbolize and to which he might relate his own poor self.

George Matheson, biblical scholar in Scotland of the nineteenth century, whose bodily eyes were blind but whose eyes of understanding saw truths that many may not see, has suggested a special meaning that may be wrapped up in Jacob's vision. The angels were "ascending and descending"; that is to say, the angels that went up toward heaven must then come down again. So if a man would have his soul be as a ladder of desire lifted up above the earth, when the angel of his better nature draws nearer to God it is not that he may stay there for his own blessing but come down again to bring the blessing of his service to the earth. That may be a hard and costly thing; and if Jacob had any awareness of this, that could be the reason for the words which are written in the Bible narrative: "He was afraid, and said, 'How awesome is this place!' "

A third fact about Jacob was that when he was committed to a purpose and caught up in an emotion, he would not get tired and give it up. If Esau was warmhearted, Jacob was deephearted. If Esau had charm, Jacob had constancy. When he left home in his flight from Esau's anger, he went to the country of his mother's kinsfolk. There he met Rachel, the daughter of Laban, and fell in love with her. Laban, harder at a bargain than Jacob once had been, demanded that Jacob work for him seven years before he could marry Rachel; and at the end of the seven years, he tried to trick him into marrying only Leah, Rachel's sister, unless he would serve for Rachel seven years more. But Jacob would not swerve from his devotion. No obstacles that Laban's craftiness could put in his way could make him betray what was in his heart. If he had to serve seven years for Rachel, he would serve seven years; and the seven years "seemed to him but a few days, because of the love he had for her."

One other incident completes the picture of Jacob. The time came when he determined to go home. Now that he would meet Esau, he must face the consequences of his guilty past. He had got the birthright. In spite of Laban he had prospered. He was returning from his exile apparently a success. So it seemed in the sight of men. But what about in the sight of God? *That* was what Jacob had to deal with now; and the reality of this is set forth in the thirty-second chapter of the Book of Genesis, in a symbolism which is dark and cryptic as we look at it first, but out of which a spiritual meaning, awesome yet healing, begins to appear. Something lays hold of Jacob, to chasten him and change him—something that was essentially within his own self, but is dramatized in the narrative as an embodied form. Old memories that he could not bury assail him, the guilt which he wished he could have forgotten rises now to haunt him like a ghost. He was walking at nightfall by the brook of Jabbok. Suddenly he found himself in the grip of a power that was terrible. A figure whose face he could not see caught him and wrestled with him, and in that desperate wrestling Jacob's thigh was put out of joint. From that hour on he would be lame. The man who once had thought that by his cleverness he could stand so tall and walk so prevailingly toward his own ends would go limping now. He could have no more pride of self-sufficiency. Instead, he must confess his wrong to Esau, and seek re-entrance into the relationship he had abused. Being ready then at last to recognize his shortcomings, he could begin to pass beyond them, and learn what God could do with a man who acknowledged that he was lame.

So he had been helped by that which had hurt him most. When the awful power which had laid hold upon his conscience had left him wounded, he still could cry out: "I will not let you go, unless you bless me." And he called the name of the place Penuel, because he said, "I have seen God face to face." No wonder then that after the long night of struggle "the sun rose upon him," even though he was "limping because of his thigh."

III

Such then is the picture of the twin brothers. In the Bible they are Esau and Jacob. But they are not in the Bible only. They are the twin possibilities in every human soul. One is the possibility which begins with all fair promise but ends in failure: the man of charm, but of a charm which is superficial; who because of his easygoing contentment with momentary satisfactions never reaches on and up to what he might attain. The other possibility is the one which at the outset seems to have no promise in it: the life which begins with obvious faults and handicaps. Who could feel anything but discouraged if that were a picture of himself?—as so many of us know for ourselves that it is.

But think again. It is not the qualities he seems to be born with, but what he does with them, that matters most in the end. Jacob may make more of life than Esau.

What then is the word for you and me who may be conscious

of our shortcomings? It is the word that speaks to us in the story of Jacob's overcoming. Look beyond today to the longer values of tomorrow; believe that in spite of our unworthiness there can be a ladder reaching up toward God; keep faithful to every high emotion; and try, as Jacob did, in all the experiences of life, even when they bring their hardest tests, to say, "I will not let you go, unless you bless me!"

2.

The Burning Bush

Who am I that I should go . . . ?
EXODUS 3:11

THOSE WORDS come from the Bible, and from one of the oldest books of the Bible at that. But how familiar they sound! They do not seem to belong to some person in a distant age. They belong to us. Have we not often said, "Who am I that some duty beyond ordinary limits should be laid on me? Who am I that I should be constrained to go out to face a difficulty or a danger which most men would never have to meet? Why should I be called upon to do what looks impossible to be done?"

Thus, with a kinship in human nature which stretches across the centuries, we echo the words of the man in the Bible. He did not want to start on a road where God wanted him to go, and neither may we. It concerns us then to consider how he felt, and to observe what happened to him afterward.

Those who know anything about the Old Testament will recognize that the man was Moses. Before his life was finished, this same Moses would become one of the great figures in human history. But at the moment when he spoke the words we have recalled it looked as though he was as far as a man could be from greatness. Two facts about him we need to understand if we would bridge that seeming contradiction, and they are these: (1) the reasons for his hesitation; (2) the power that carried him through.

I

It seemed to Moses that he had a right to hesitate and to flinch from the demand which was laid upon him, for a whole regiment of reasons.

He had been born in Egypt, the child of a Hebrew mother and father, and the Hebrews—the people of Israel—were slaves to the Egyptian Pharaoh. He had been hidden by his mother at a time when the Pharaoh, fearful of imagined danger to Egypt's safety from this slave people, had issued a savage order for the killing of their boy babies. Then an incredible thing happened. The little child Moses was found by the daughter of Pharaoh himself as she went out to bathe one day in the Nile River; and at the impulse of her woman's heart, she took him up and had him carried to the royal palace, with no one in Pharaoh's circle knowing who he was. Under that protection he grew up, while the people of whose blood he was still toiled in Egyptian bondage.

Life and all its prospects could have been smooth for Moses. He might have settled down into the soft privilege and ease which had so strangely come to him. But he could not wholly do it. Something deep within him troubled him. By adoption he was the son of Pharaoh's daughter, but more profoundly he was a son of Israel. The fate of the Israelitish people was like a magnetic force that reached out to draw him into its involvement. One day as he passed a group of Israelites at their forced labor he saw one of them lashed by an Egyptian taskmaster. In sudden indignation, he struck the Egyptian—struck him with such imperious strength that the Egyptian fell down dead. In horror at what he had impulsively done, he hid the body in the sand; and he looked this way and that to discover whether any other of Pharaoh's guards had seen the killing. Only some of the Israelites, it appeared, had been witnesses of it; and certainly none of them—he thought—would ever tell, or be anything but grateful to him who had come to the defense of their fellow Israelite.

But the next day he had the shock of a different realization. When he tried to restrain an Israelitish worker who was in a rage with one of his companions, the man's hot resentment flared into a challenge: "Who made you a prince or judge over us? Do you mean to kill me as you killed the Egyptian?" Then—as the swift narrative in the Book of Exodus continues—"Moses was afraid, and thought, 'Surely the thing is known.' " Before long it was known; and the account in the Book of Exodus ends with this grim sentence, "When Pharaoh heard of it, he sought to kill Moses."

So there was nothing for Moses now but to get out of Egypt as quickly as he could. He fled to the desolate country that lay beyond the peninsula of Sinai. There presently he found himself herding goats for a man who had given him shelter—herding goats instead of living in privilege at the favor of Pharaoh's daughter. It did not seem that he was much of a figure now.

But one day in the stark desert loneliness he had a vision. He saw a bush that seemed to be on fire, and yet was not consumed. As we read the description in the biblical account, we cannot say we know the meaning of that burning bush. Probably Moses at that moment could not have told the meaning of it either. But this perhaps is what it symbolized: the fact that down deep in Moses' soul was the compulsion of belief that somehow, sometime, his life was meant to be significant. It was the inextinguishable restlessness which other human spirits have known and may know now, even in times when we cannot tell what it is or what it may lead to: the flame of conscience and unfinished duty burning, burning, refusing to sink down into ashes, holding us still in the circle of its power even in the place of escape where we had supposed it would not be.

Then this haunting suggestion of the bush that burned with fire, yet was not consumed, became explicit. In Moses' heart before he fled from Egypt there had been a spark of heroic purpose: to champion the cause of the oppressed people of his own blood, somehow to set them free. Now the compulsion of that purpose came back to him as a voice direct from God: "Behold, the cry of the people of Israel has come to me, and I have seen the oppression with which the Egyptians oppress them. Come, I will send you to Pharaoh that you may bring forth my people, the sons of Israel, out of Egypt."

Thus two ranges of facts came into shattering collision: on the one hand, Moses' recognition of what he ought to try to do; on the other hand, his appalled consciousness of how impossible it seemed that he could ever do it. Pharaoh was king of Egypt, with power of life and death. Pharaoh already hated him and had sought to kill him. Yet he, Moses, was to appear before Pharaoh and tell him in the name of God to let the people of Israel go! No wonder he began to answer the voice of God with the voice of his own consternation and confusion.

It was not only Pharaoh that he would have to deal with. He would have to convince the people of Israel that it was by divine commission that he was coming to their help. But how could he convince them when he himself knew so little about God? "If I come to the people of Israel and say to them, 'The God of your fathers has sent me to you,' and they ask me, 'What is his name?' what shall I say to them?"

That question expressed a kind of frustration that did not end with Moses. In every generation men have stumbled at going ahead with a duty their conscience knew to be the will of God, because they thought they could not put into convincing words what nevertheless they deeply knew. They were afraid they might be embarrassed in speaking for God if they could not give smooth explanations about God. "I am not schooled in religious matters. Somebody who knows theological language will do better than I."

Moses came back to his same excuse in further words: "Oh, my Lord, I am not eloquent; either heretofore or since thou hast spoken to thy servant, for I am slow of speech and of tongue." Then the Lord said to him, "Who has made man's mouth? Who makes him dumb, or deaf, or seeing, or blind? Is it not I, the Lord? Now therefore go, and I will be with your mouth and teach you what you shall speak."

Other difficulties also Moses brought forward, until he had run out of specific reasons why the commission God sought to lay on him could not be accomplished. Maybe it could be carried out by the right man somehow. But all the same Moses stuck to his plea that *he* was not the man to do it. Wouldn't the Lord please send somebody else? Who am I that *I* should go?

In our present time much is written and parroted concerning "the power of positive thinking." That may become only a glib prescription, but at its best it can have value in it. More value certainly than in the negative thinking which was about to paralyze Moses. If he had persisted in that kind of feebleness and evasion, he would have ended as a discreditable failure. But something different happened. This Moses sitting glumly in the wilderness comes out of the wilderness. This man, who imagined that he could not amount to anything, gets up and goes back to where something tremendous is waiting for him to do. In spite of his fears, he will confront Pharaoh. In spite of his doubts as to whether they will listen, he will carry God's promise of deliverance to the people of Israel. And before his life is over, he will lead that people—notwithstanding difficulties and discouragements beyond what he could have imagined—out of Egypt, out of slavery, to the Promised Land.

II

What made the transformation?
Three things:
1. In the first place, the vision of the burning bush jolted Moses into a new self-appraisal. What if the destined possibility of his life—like the bush—was still on fire and the promise of it not consumed? In the compulsion of that vision Moses stood in awe, and began to see

the truth: the whole truth, and not the enfeebling little fragment of reality which he had treated as the whole of what existed. It was true that there were facts which had seemed strong enough to destroy him, but it was also true that there was something else on which he could build. He was guilty of the death of the Egyptian; yes. He had put himself in lasting peril; yes. By all those in Egypt who looked only on the surface of the picture he was hated and maligned. Nevertheless, who and what was he at heart? A man who had been moved by a passionate championship of the oppressed. A man who when he struck the Egyptian taskmaster had not meant to kill him. A man who even in the violence he had committed had been moved only by desire to help those who needed help. All this in the sight of God he was, and in the strength of *this*—and not in the paralysis of his fears and liabilities—he must begin to live.

The crises of men's decisions are always different in their particular circumstances, but some principles are always true. One is the fact which Moses was brought to understand: that a man must set up the flag of some affirmative conception of himself, so that all the little discouraged and scattered elements of his possible power may rally round it. "Who am I? Well, at least I do not need to be the shadow of other people's opinions, good or bad. I am the man God made, and made not to be an acquiescent failure. Some assets of ability, of character and of experience I do possess; and on *those* I propose to build, come sun, or rain, or storm." That in effect was what Moses learned to say in the wilderness, and that was the first awakening which made him not stay in the wilderness but come out.

The experience which Moses had to deal with was no far-off and unrelated thing. In essential parallel it may be reflected as long as human life goes on. In 1921 Franklin D. Roosevelt was struck down by infantile paralysis. He might have said to himself, "Fate has dealt me a bitter blow. My energies are crippled. In the old sense of full activity, I am out of the race. Well then, so be it. I have enough to live on. Let me shrug my shoulders and settle down to nurse myself and let the world go by."

That was exactly what some who were solicitous for his comfort wanted him to do. On the other hand was another urging: to let himself be nominated for the governorship of New York in a critical political campaign in which men told him that his enlistment was essential. *He* have to do that? He with his paralysis accept the cruel physical strain which he would have to face? And for what likelihood? He had been defeated when he ran for public office the last time, for the Vice-Presidency in 1920. How could he summon up enough strength now to make another effort anything but useless? Twice he said No to those who were trying to persuade him. But at last he made what seemed the costly decision. He dared to take the affirmative chance of what his possibilities of achievement still might be, and that risk became the open gateway into the part which he would play in history.

2. A willingness to listen to the larger call, a vision of the burning bush that would not be consumed: that first. Then out of these there came to Moses, as there may come also to other men, the specific recognition of a great cause and its power to give a man strength beyond his own.

Moses had had a foregleam of that in Egypt. He might have wrapped himself in the privileges which had come to him in Pharaoh's court, and troubled himself with no greater concern. But something else spoke to his sympathy and his conscience. The people of Israel were his people. And he belonged to them. How could he stand aside and do nothing when they were oppressed?

That is what he had begun to feel on the day when he saw the cruelty of the Egyptian taskmaster and when he struck his fateful blow. Now he knew that it was there at the side of the oppressed that he had to be. So in spite of his evasions he obeyed the compelling voice. He went back to Egypt to confront Pharaoh with the sovereign demand, "Let my people go!"

From that time on Moses was bound up with the fate of Israel. This would bring him burdens of responsibility and sometimes resistance which seemed to be greater than any man could cope with, but it was because of the strength which this called forth in him that he would attain to greatness.

First there was the struggle of wills between himself and Pharaoh. It was no wonder that "Pharaoh's heart was hardened, and he would not listen." The amazing fact was that Moses got into Pharaoh's presence at all, and was able to stand before him without being thrown into prison instead. Little by little he brought to bear on Pharaoh an awesome moral force that Pharaoh could not cope with. At first the king resisted Moses' demands with angry scorn, and once in fury he cried out, "Get away from me; take heed to yourself; never see my face again, for in the day you see my face you shall die!"

But Moses was not daunted. Day after day he came back, and repeatedly he forced from Pharaoh concessions which Pharaoh, when his mind had changed, retracted. Then Moses dared the ultimate action. Pharaoh or no Pharaoh, he would take the people of Israel out of Egypt. Secretly they were organized and instructed. In the night they kept the solemn feast of Passover, and under the cover of darkness they began their exodus—with the rumble of Pharaoh's pursuing chariots sounding in their ears from behind them before they could get across the protecting arm of the Red Sea.

The marvel which the Book of Exodus recounts of Pharaoh's chariots caught and destroyed in the shifting waters of the sea ended the threat from Pharaoh. But Moses' task, and his troubles, had only begun.

To espouse a great cause does not mean that the pursuit of it will be glamorous. Moses had committed himself to a brave and selfless venture: to lead the people of Israel out of slavery into a new life. But if he had imagined that the people would always respond with understanding and gratitude, he was to learn a fact so different that it could be staggering. Those he was trying to help could be critical, cantankerous, and complaining. He would have to face what everyone dedicated to public service may always have to face: a resistance so stupid and so stubborn that a man might be tempted to ask himself, "Why was I ever so foolish as to think that there was anything I could do?" To confront *that* question would require in Moses more steadfastness and continuing courage than he had had need of in confronting Pharaoh.

The exodus had hardly begun when Moses got his first evidence of how fickle and feeble human beings can show themselves to be. When the first report came that Pharaoh's chariots were pursuing, this was the lamentation Moses had to listen to. "Is it because there are no graves in Egypt that you have taken us away to die in the wilderness? What have you done to us, in bringing us out of Egypt? Is not this what we said to you in Egypt, 'Let us alone and let us serve the Egyptians'? For it would have been better to serve the Egyptians than to die in the wilderness."

When they had not died but had escaped, they still complained. Food ran low, they blamed Moses again. "Would that we had died by the hand of the Lord in the land of Egypt, when we sat by the fleshpots and ate bread to the full; for you have brought us out into this wilderness to kill this whole assembly with hunger." Later, when they had got to a place where there was no water, they said that all that Moses had done in bringing them out of Egypt was "to kill us and our children and our cattle with thirst."

So, every time they encountered any hardship, the people blamed Moses for it all, and at last they were ready to try mutiny. Moses' own brother and sister, Aaron and Miriam, broke out with their petulant question, "Has the Lord spoken only through Moses? Has he not spoken through us also?" And when one day there seemed to be danger from hostile tribes along their road, the whole assembly raised a loud cry, and they said, "Our wives and our little ones will become a prey. Let us choose a captain, and go back to Egypt."

Profiles in Courage, which President John F. Kennedy wrote when he was in the Senate, is modern evidence of the inspired resolution a man in public leadership must have if he is to hold to some great purpose he has seen and intends to follow even when the crowd will try to howl him down. That takes no mere momentary courage, but the kind of unbreakable strength which belongs only to the man who is linked with something larger than himself. That was what had happened to Moses—and can happen in any generation to a man who has been gripped by some invincible ideal. He has dedicated himself to the long-range good, and he will pursue *that*, no matter if the shallow and the selfish want some mean little immediate satisfaction for their appetites instead. "I have come home to tell you the truth," said Senator George W. Norris to his constituents in Nebraska at a moment when his popularity and his political life were both at stake.[1] Because he had integrity, and a clean commitment to what he believed was right, he had the inner power which no outer pressure could affect.

3. Beyond what we have thought of already, there is the highest and the final fact. Moses came out of the wilderness of his indecision because he was led to a braver self-appraisal, and because he was seized upon by the attraction of a heroic cause. But that cause might not have been able to sustain him except that through it he found—God.

Confronted with the unresponsiveness and the near-rebellion of the people he sought to lead, Moses prayed: "If thy presence will not go with me, do not carry us up from here." It had to be true of him, as would be written long afterward in the Epistle to the Hebrews, that "he endured as seeing him who is invisible." He learned what was echoed in our own generation in the words which King George VI of England, at one of the dark moments of the Second World War, repeated: "I said to the man who stood at the gate of the year, 'Give me a light that I may tread safely into the unknown.' But he answered, 'Put your hand into the hand of God. That will be to you better than a light, and safer than a known way.' "

[1] *Profiles in Courage* (New York: Pocket Books, Inc., 1963), p. 171.

How does God become a reality? Not in words. Not in speculation and argument. No, but in obedience to some summons which enlists what is truest and bravest in a man's soul. When he follows that in action, then God is made manifest in the energies beyond his own which begin to flow into him.

Remember now what seemed at first the baffling answer which God gave to Moses when Moses asked what he should say to the people in Egypt, if they should demand to know who was the God he spoke for and what was his name. "God said to Moses, *I am who I am*"; or, as the marginal note in the Revised Standard Version translates the Hebrew original, "*I will be what I will be.*" That is to say, the reality of the divine cannot be cramped into a definition. It is revealed in the life experience of the man who reaches out to God. God is the whole profound meaning of life that is and that is to be, as this meaning gradually and continually is set forth. All great memories of the past, all remorse for failure or gratitude for faithfulness, all deeds of today or hopes for tomorrow—these are part of the continuous impact of God on human life. It was as though the divine voice had said to Moses: "You cannot know me by anything I tell you now. You cannot recognize me, as you imagine, by any fleeting signs that I might give. You will know me only as day is added to day; and from every day lived in loyalty to the highest you then know, you gather your increasing understanding of what life and God can mean."

The reason some people never learn the reality of God and the power that God might bring to them is because they have not let their lives expand to anything large enough to need him. A beast can sleep and feed with no consciousness of God. A man can do the same. He can go about the narrow business of those pursuits which minister to his immediate requirements, live for himself and his small advantage, and never remember God. But if his thought and desire are bent upon accomplishments beyond the utmost resources which he has within himself, if he tries to answer the voice like that from the burning bush which brings its challenge to what may be costly service, then he must have God go with him if he would go at all.

What may happen then to any man's soul is like what may happen for one who stands on the ground by an inlet from the ocean where great tides rise and fall. The tides will not concern him if all he wants is to stay on shore. But if his heart is bent upon some great voyage, he will be looking out beyond the inlet for the mighty reinforcement which must come from the ocean deeps. He will trust and wait for the tides of God which can flood beneath the stranded ship of his own insufficiency, to lift him over the shallows, and to carry him rejoicingly out to sea.

"Who am I that I should go?" That is the question which a man—or a woman—may ask at first when there comes some startling suggestion of a work to be done and the need of someone who will try to do it: some entrenched evil to be confronted and withstood, some helpless human group to be defended, some unpopular program for social betterment to be believed in and set on foot. "I am not the one for that," we may be tempted to say; and in saying so condemn ourselves to littleness. But the one who in spite of doubt and hesitation goes out to give all he has to the best he knows will find the enlargement of life which God gives to those who listen to the summoning word.

3.

From Ashes to God

To grant to those who mourn in Zion—
To give them a garland instead of ashes,
The oil of gladness instead of mourning,
The mantle of praise instead of a faint spirit.

ISAIAH 61:3

SOMETIMES MEN in the ministry may fall into the error of supposing that their function is something quite special and separate. They are to study about God from the Bible and from other books, and then tell people what the people do not know. They are to preach and the congregation is to listen. Are they not the experts in spiritual matters?

But the truth is different. The Holy Spirit does not speak through the lips of preachers only—or through their lives either. The Holy Spirit's message may come through men and women in every ordinary place: men and women of no ecclesiastical status but to whom in some deep experience of life there have come convictions which possess an instant power such as utterances from pulpits do not always equal. It behooves every minister to be sensitive to what all human beings round him may have to say to him. They can bring him glimpses of how God's reality is manifest which will give a new warmth and wideness of understanding to what he tries to preach on Sunday, and a new mutuality of spiritual comradeship wherever he is in touch with human souls. So as a minister he will not commit the grievous fault of assuming that his special training means that he does not need to learn. By some spontaneous word from an unexpected person he may be made aware of a truth of God which by himself he would have never known.

It is within the framework of facts like those that what I am about to express is set. Such message as may be now conveyed came first not from the pulpit to the pew but from the pew to the pulpit: no, not from the pew either; rather, from one who may not have been in a church at all, but who in the shock of life had learned something which the pulpit must listen to and try to interpret.

At the beginning of the 1930s there fell upon the United States a shattering financial depression which altered the face of existence for innumerable people. One day there came to me a young artist who, like many others of her group, faced devastating hardships in that period when most people had to spend all that they possessed for bare necessities, and therefore had nothing left with which to patronize the arts. This particular artist felt the calamity of those years as keenly as anyone could. It had meant the loss of patrons, the loss of a studio, the loss of the satisfaction of being creatively at work. It had meant at length going on relief. Yet under all these things her spirit had not been broken. On the contrary, it had gained something which many of us in what seem happier circumstances never gain. And this is what she said to me. "If I could write a book, I would call it by this title, 'From Ashes to God.' " Then after a moment she went on. "You must be annihilated, stepped on, I don't mean any halfway stuff. Then when everything in you seems to have been extinguished, a new little flame is somehow lighted which grows and grows and can never be put out. That flame is God."

Therefore I have given to what is written here the title which I think would be hers, "From Ashes to God." One of the special seasons of the Church year is the period of Lent. It is with Ash Wednesday that Lent begins, and Lent is full of the thought of those deep valleys of humiliation into which the human spirit often must go down. It echoes with an everlasting *De profundis*. But it is not in any special season only that there can come to us a realization of the distresses which life may have to meet. That is an element which has existed in human experience as far back as we can trace the consciousness of man.

Turn and look back along the far dim vistas of the Old Testament. There on the threshold of history is Jacob, beholding his vision of God from the desert of his lonely and embittered flight, bowing his head and saying, "How dreadful is this place!" There is Moses, transfixed with awe before the burning bush. There is the psalmist, crying, "Have mercy upon me." There is Paul, in a moment of near-despair exclaiming, "O wretched man that I am! who shall deliver me from the body of this death?" It is the echo of a human experience which knows what it means to be clothed with the sackcloth of defeat and desolation and to see life turned to ashes in its hands.

But the glory of the religious message is that, although life may begin with the stark, sheer realism of our most difficult human facts, it does not end there. It ends rather with redemption. It begins with human weakness, but it goes on to God. It begins with ashes, but it can end with beauty. In place of mourning, it brings the oil of gladness. In place of a faint spirit, the mantle of praise.

In this mood, therefore, let us follow our thought now, the thought that leads "from ashes to God."

I

In the first place, we shall consider deliverance from defeat.

Most obviously there is the defeat in the field of material circumstances. It was this kind of defeat which seemed to be involved in the instance of the artist of whom I spoke just now. In spite of anything and everything she could do, the facts of her world had gone against her. It looked as though every legitimate hope and ambition had been destroyed. What could be more devastating than a life in which its most eager and creative purpose seemed to be frustrated at every turn? How could it be possible that that life with circumstances remaining as they were could emerge into victory?

The most immediate element in the answer will seem strange and contradictory. The way to overcome defeat may be to accept defeat. It is only when you have been annihilated, she said, that you find God.

Is that only a verbal flourish? Is it merely a manufactured illusion by which one manages to ignore the cruel fact? No, it is not! An immortal truth is shining there. It *is* true that when a soul enters most completely into its defeat, disguises nothing, evades nothing, accepts the full consequences of life as life really is, that soul may be on the threshold of its larger triumph.

This fact is not theoretical. We can see it embodied in great figures both of the past and of the present. Look, for example, at the biblical figure of Joseph. You will remember that beautiful, dramatic story of his life as it is unfolded in the pages of the Book of Genesis. In the beginning, Joseph is the lad who seems destined for sure success. Every chance of life is loaded in his favor. He is sure of himself, ambitious, overconfident, aggressive. He dreams his dreams of greatness and does not hesitate to make known his confidence that they will be fulfilled. Then comes disaster. His brothers, angered by his superiority, turn upon him, strip him of his rich clothes, sell him into Egypt as a slave. There in Egypt,

Joseph tastes the ultimate dregs of bitterness. He is the victim of false accusations and is put into prison with men condemned for common crimes. But what does he do? He does not sit down idly and bemoan his lot. Instead he meets his disasters with a spirit that grows increasingly intelligent, self-critical, steadfast, and determined. He cannot help his trial from being a terrible and fiery thing. But he makes that fire into a refining furnace, in the midst of which all that had been small and selfish in his nature is burned away. The ashes are there; but they are the ashes of his dross, and out of them comes the gold of his new and better self.

He emerges presently from the prison because he had made himself fit to seize the opportunity which could set him free. He becomes a viceroy of Pharaoh, and the servant of a nation. And in the highest scene of his career, when through a strange turn of events, those same brothers of his who had sold him into slavery stand before him as victims of famine begging for food, and he the viceroy of Pharaoh is revealed to them as Joseph the brother whom they have sold, this man, looking at his life, sees how the ashes of it had been turned into glory, and remembering how dark the past had been, tells them no longer to consider it as an evil, for "it was not you," he says, "that sent me hither. It was God."

Or look at a nearer figure. There is Paul, the brilliant scholar, a Roman citizen, a man born to privilege and endowed with the promise of the great influence which his intellectual power commanded among his people. But this man undergoes a tremendous spiritual experience. He accepts as his Master Jesus who had been put to death upon a cross. He loses everything he thought he had valued most—his standing among his own people, his prestige, the kind of life of sheltered privilege which once he had enjoyed. He is to be hated, persecuted, threatened again and again with death; but his soul was born anew. The man he had been was in fact annihilated. But another man was fashioned who had on him the mark of the everlasting power of God. He was not framing any idle words when he spoke of those who "out of weakness are made strong" and of those who may be dying, and yet "behold, we live." He too had gone through a period when most of what he originally thought precious had turned to ashes; but in the ashes he had found God.

But do you say that these after all are far-off figures and belong in what seems sometimes the almost legendary literature of superhuman souls? If you think so, come down to our own century. One of the great figures in modern medicine was Edward L. Trudeau, who perhaps more than any other single man gave hope and courage to multitudes who have had to face the terror of tuberculosis. He was cut down in the prime of life and doomed, as it seemed at the beginning, to a useless invalidism; his expanding career in New York City ended, and he himself exiled to the Adirondacks. But he turned his disaster into opportunity and became a pioneer in a new, hopeful way of dealing with the dread disease:

It took me a long time to learn, imperfectly though it be, that acquiescence is the only way for the tuberculous invalid to conquer fate. To cease to rebel and struggle, and to learn to be content with part of a loaf when one cannot have a whole loaf, though a hard lesson to learn, is good philosophy for the tuberculous invalid, and to his astonishment he often finds that what he considers the half loaf, when acquiesced in, proves most satisfying. It was many years, however, before I learned this great lesson, but when once learned it made life fuller and happier.

And he wrote again of those influences which are

still making life precious to me every hour; full of the aspirations and ceaseless strivings of the spirit for expression in worship, ever groping to know God, and ever sustained through long periods of gloom by too swiftly fading glimpses of the Heavenly Vision,

and his autobiography closes with these great words:

> After all, I can truly say
> "With their triumphs and their glories and the rest,
> Love is best."[1]

Is there any doubt that that man went from ashes to God?

Also there is another voice that we may listen to, which came from amidst the most cruel sufferings of the Second World War. Martin Niemoeller, once a submarine commander but later an evangelical pastor preaching the Christian gospel in defiance of Adolf Hitler, was arrested and put on trial for his life. From his cell in the Berlin prison, he wrote to his wife.

I should like to tell you that I am not only unbroken after six weeks of imprisonment but am full of joy and gratitude for God's gracious guidance. . . . It is one of our Lord's unfathomable truths that His trust upholds

[1] Edward Livingston Trudeau, *An Autobiography* (Garden City, N.Y.: Doubleday, Page & Co., 1916), pp. 74, 321.

our peace of mind in all situations of life. . . . I am now resting in peace after the abundant turmoil of the last few years, and am waiting, patient and full of confidence, if the Lord will again need me for service outside these walls.

There is a beautiful suggestion in a verse of one of the Pilgrim Psalms—the psalms which were sung by the throngs in Israel who went up to Jerusalem for the great festivals of the religious year:

> As they go through the valley of Baca
> They make it a place of springs.

Or as the Hebrew words were translated by Miles Coverdale in the version which has come down to us in the Book of Common Prayer,

> Who going through the vale of misery
> use it for a well.

The valley of Baca was evidently an arid region of broken rock and bare sand and burnt earth which lay somewhere on the road to Jerusalem. It was a weary stretch on the journey for pilgrims to pass through. It might have been—as some areas on the road of life for every generation may seem to be—a vale of misery. But the pilgrims were going up to the Holy City; and if the valley of Baca were a necessary stage in getting there, then the valley itself could become "a place of springs." In the midst of what might have been discouragement, new courage; in the midst of difficulty, the fountains of new purpose and recruited strength.

So perhaps we have said enough to make it plain that gallant souls can so deal with hard facts as to find in them a well, so rise from ashes as to be more aware of God.

But there must be those who realize that their worst distresses are not with reference to what outward circumstances may have visited upon them. Their worst distresses come not from any hostile fate but from inward failures. By some decisive sin, or more probably by little slacknesses and compromises and by almost unperceived degrees, they have lost the integrity of their souls. Once they were aware of all sorts of beautiful aspirations that were sweet within their spirits like flowers within a garden. Now there is no garden any more, but only the arid place from which the promise has faded and over which there has settled the dust of bitter memories and regrets. Who is there here today who will not confess that this is true for at least some part of the ground of his soul?

It is good to remember that the words of the prophet Isaiah were spoken first to men and women who were in exile. They had been separated, not only through their own sins but through the sins of their fathers, from the relationships that once had given life its dignity and beauty. They were living in a land where they seemed cut off from God. Their plight may be ours today. It is not only that we feel our individual shortcomings, but that we know that we are involved in the results of widespread and ancient social sins, the selfishness of whole communities, the hard materialism of much of the civilization which we in part have built and in part have accepted and approved—its inhumanities, its ruthlessness toward many finer values in its pursuit for gain, its specious power-politics which have brought us the evil of two world wars and the ghastly possibility of another as the ultimate Armageddon. All these things and the results of them we share. It is only natural that many should be oppressed today by the fear lest our whole existence may turn to ashes. The blight of our moral mistakes lies on us and on our world.

How shall we emerge from this shadow? By confessing, first of all, that we are in it, by looking straight into the face of existing facts, by dealing honestly with our personal and social iniquities, by crying like the psalmist, "Against thee, thee only, have I sinned, and done that which is evil in thy sight." By no less genuine a process than this can we get free. We cannot cure our inner unrest. No more can we hope to deliver our world from its increasing perils, unless we are honest enough and thoroughgoing enough to realize our need for moral understanding, for repentance and regeneration. In this inner world, as in the outward world of material fortune, the prophetic words of the young artist are true. "There must be no halfway stuff. You must be annihilated before you can be born again." And the message which comes to us is that this miracle can come true. If the soul of a man and the conscience of a nation really wants to get rid of the evil that distresses it, there is a divine grace which will lift the burden of that evil off. If we want to save our civilization from the influences which now are bringing toward it the shadow of its possible doom, it may not be too late. The crucial matter for us is that we should look into our own life and ask what ignorance, indifference, or evil may be there which contributes to the destructive forces of our time. As individual citizens, notwithstanding the seeming unimportance of single persons, do in the long run shape the public opinion and determine the choices of a nation, therefore each one of us must contribute as far as in us lies to the steady thinking and the clean will that may make this country an instrument of the saving purposes of God. When we have let the flame of spiritual sincerity reduce some of our pride and self-assertion into ashes, we may find the oil of gladness instead of mourning, and a mantle of praise instead of a faint spirit.

II

Up to this point we have been speaking of finding God through defeat. It remains that we should speak of finding God through and beyond our seeming victories.

There was an old custom in the early Church which had a beautiful symbolism. On the altar every Ash Wednesday there were sprinkled ashes, and the particular significance of those ashes lay in the fact of what they came from. They were the ashes gathered from the burning of the palms which had been used in the triumphant worship of Palm Sunday in the year before. Those palms represented a spiritual enthusiasm. The multitude that crowded round Jesus as he entered Jerusalem waved branches of the palms to show that they welcomed him. They were expressing as best they could a loyalty which they thought they felt. But when anyone considers the events of the days that followed Palm Sunday, one sees how fickle and ineffective that welcome was. Jesus, round whose way the crowd shouted their hosannas, was the same Jesus whom those crowds suffered five days later to be put to death. So in the retrospect the palms became the symbol of mingled pride and shame. They represented an ideal that people wanted to be true to, but they represented also a commitment in which they pitifully failed. They represented the desire for something better, but at the same time they expressed the fact that that better was not good enough.

If, therefore, we would understand the full meaning of passing "from ashes to God," let us remember that the ashes may need to be not only our defeats, but also those things which with too easy confidence we have imagined to be our victories. Possibly in this last year we have taken some stand which represented a new religious loyalty. Some perhaps in these past months may have become members of a church, because you definitely wanted to "confess the faith of Christ crucified and manfully to fight under his banner against sin, the world, and the devil" unto your life's end. Some of you have made your own less conspicuous but no less real resolutions to be better members of the church to which you already belong. Some of you have identified yourselves with influences in the community that make for righteousness and mercy, and you have devoted a definite part of your time and energy to these commitments.

They represent the palms by which you have expressed your would-be identification with the spirit of Christ and his larger entrance into your life. But if you have been growing in spiritual perception and sensitiveness you will realize that those commitments are not enough. You will see how often your loyalties have been ineffective and your identification with the cause of Christ has failed when the real test came. If we are to gain, therefore, the real power of God, which is our hope and possibility, we must be willing to treat those little partial victories as though they were ashes too. We must be careful lest we fall into the pride and the self-satisfaction which can be the greatest blight on spiritual growth. We need to say: "O Lord, here are the evidences of whatever desires of mine in the days past have been true and good. Here are the things I wanted to do. Here are the ideals to which I wanted to be loyal. Here are the palms with which in honesty of heart I sought to welcome thee. I would not forget these nor belittle them. I am thankful that I did have them in my hands. But I know they are not enough. I want to go beyond the inadequate faithfulness which they represented. It is out of the ashes of these that I want to find the new and fuller flame of God."

Thus it becomes true, you see, that the progress of our spiritual life is no mere turning of a wheel that always in its revolution comes back to the point at which it started. On the contrary, it is like the climbing of a mountain. In the ascent there may be many lesser hills, and many valleys in between. We come to the crest of one; and as we near it, we see above us the crest of another, and when we have come there we imagine that we have come to the end of the climb. But then from the actual top of the hill we see that the climb is not ended. Indeed, it may be that it is only well begun. We have to go down into another valley and then up another hill, and beyond that may lie other hills and other valleys before we come to the ultimate crest. But the climbing of each new hill is no mere repetition of the climbing already accomplished. Each hill is a little higher than the former one. Each ascent is a little nearer to the final goal. There will be many moments when we have to recognize, in the words which Winston Churchill used at one of the critical moments of his people's struggle, that we are not at "the beginning of the end," but at least we may be able to say that we are at "the end of the beginning." So it is only as each partial climb is left behind that we come at last to the mountaintop and know that we have achieved.

4.

When a Soul Commits Suicide

> Therefore Saul took his own sword,
> and fell upon it.
>
> I SAMUEL 31:4

HERE IS the grim climax of what might have been a great career. Saul, the king of Israel, has been defeated by the Philistines. On the battlefield of Mount Gilboa his army is broken and scattered. Three of his sons, including the gallant Jonathan, have been slain. He himself has been wounded by Philistine arrows; and as his foes press in to finish him, the bitterness of his defeat is worse to him than death. "Draw your sword, and thrust me through with it," he commanded his armor-bearer; and when the armor-bearer shrank from that appalling order and would not kill him, Saul took his own sword and killed himself.

Such was the physical act, and it was tragic enough; but it symbolized another tragedy which was deeper. It was not only on Mount Gilboa that Saul committed suicide. For a long time, in ways less visible but no less deadly, he had been doing that. He was a man who had held in his hand the sword of magnificent endowments, but he had turned that sword against himself. He had dealt death to his soul by his own perverted possibilities.

Nor has he been alone. Others—yesterday, today, and tomorrow— may be like Saul. What happens to them, and in them, may not be so dramatic as the story of Saul. But it may be as real, and as somber; for it embodies again the tragedy of that which ought to have been noble going down to ignoble self-destruction. It may not seem a matter of much significance when a life which never had any conspicuous promise comes to a shrunken end. But there is reason for mourning when a man who has had everything to live for, and to serve with, stands at the end with nothing in his hand but a sword stained with the blood of his better self.

Thinking of him then not only in the framework of an ancient world but as reappearing in the world we know and live in, let us consider the figure of Saul in what was at first his greatness, and then the fault which left him at last with all his greatness gone.

I

It would be difficult to imagine a man more attractive than the Saul who appears at the beginning of the Bible narrative. The times were troubled. The life of the people of Israel was confused and leaderless. Then the old prophet Samuel discovered a young man of the tribe of Benjamin who seemed to him to be destined by the Lord to answer the people's need. He had not sought any honors. When he learned that Samuel was about to call him to great responsibility, he took himself off where he hoped that he would not be found. When he was found, and Samuel presented him to the people, it was seen that physically he was superb, "taller than any of the people from his shoulders upward."

As he was tall in stature, so it appeared—which was more important —that there was a tallness in his spirit, a magnanimity that would not easily stoop to mean considerations. When he was chosen by Samuel for leadership, "some worthless fellows," as the First Book of Samuel calls them, said: "How can this man save us?" and the narrative goes on, "They despised him and brought him no present." Although Saul made no angry comment, it might have been supposed that he would remember with resentment and express that resentment when the right time came. But the fact was otherwise. Not long after that day when the "worthless fellows" had despised him, Saul had his first test in action. A marauding band of Ammonites attacked the village of Jabesh-gilead, and held the people for ransom at a ferocious price. Up to then there had been no strong force in Israel that could have promised rescue. But when Saul heard of what had happened, there flamed in him a moral indignation which was like a spreading fire. He summoned men from all the region to his side, and he sent word to the people of Jabesh-gilead, "Tomorrow, by the time the sun is hot, you shall have deliverance." His deed was as good as his word. He did drive off the Ammonites in a sweeping victory, and set the terrified village free. And then what? An impulse to exploit what he had done, and especially to settle accounts with the little clique who had despised him? No. His fighting men were ready for exactly that. "Who is it that said, 'Shall Saul reign over us?'" they demanded. "Bring the men, that we may put them to death." But Saul answered, "Not a man shall be put to death this day, for today the Lord has wrought deliverance in Israel."

So he could be forbearing. He could be affectionate, too. A little later there came into Saul's life the young David, who had tended his father's sheep in the fields of Bethlehem, but who also was skillful in playing on the lyre. There was a charm and freshness about David to which something sensitive in Saul responded. He sent word to David's father that he wanted to keep David in his service, for "he loved him greatly."

Thus in Saul there was much that every man who knew him held in honor. And back of all that the whole people could see was admirable, there was the deeper fact which the thoughtful could recognize as most important. Saul seemed to be a dedicated man. Samuel had called him to service in the name of God, and it was in God's name that he had responded. It was recorded that "God gave him another heart," and there came to him a moment of such spiritual exaltation that the people exclaimed, "Is Saul also among the prophets?" He had shown no sign of seeking personal glory. After he had won the fight against the Ammonite marauders he had not claimed personal victory. "Today the Lord," he had said, "*the Lord* has wrought deliverance in Israel."

What other side of the story, then, could there be? What cloud of possible tragedy could be gathering low down on the horizon? Certainly there seemed to be none. Here, so far, was a career of conspicuous promise. This man, handsome, strong, courageous and commanding, how could he have ahead of him anything but a high fulfillment of the record he had begun to make? His great possibilities were like a sword in his hand, to be used for unlimited service. Who could foresee that the sword would be used for suicide?

II

Where, then, was the turning point for Saul? Not in any moment of recognized failure, but in the building up of too much success; not because of weakness but because of power, and the obsession which began to grow in him to keep the power that he had.

It can be a deadly thing when a man—in ways so subtle and so gradual that they may be almost hidden from himself—begins to lose his commitment to that which is larger than himself. That is what happened to Saul. At first he had meant to be the servant of the will of God as the prophet Samuel had inspired him to understand it. Then, as he became more conscious of his own authority, he began to make decisions which would heighten his own prestige. He could tell himself plausible reasons for what he did, but the fact was that he had an uneasy conscience. The moral issues at stake, as they are reflected in the Book of Samuel, are sometimes not clear to our modern thinking; but what *is* clear is that the prophet Samuel judged Saul to be guilty of spiritual disobedience, and threatened to denounce him as unworthy of the kingship to which he had been anointed.

From that time on, Saul's energies turned into a different channel. He had wanted Samuel's blessing, but if he had to lose it, he would go on his way without it. Samuel had made him king, and king he was determined to remain. He had started out to serve God and the people. God and the people still ought to be served—but not without reference to the importance of Saul. He would maintain his own eminence, and so much the worse for anyone who threatened it.

There is a kind of all-out determination which can make a man magnificent. If he is linked with some great loyalty, then all the strength he can bring to bear makes him the greater person. But if it becomes his primary purpose to serve himself, then all his energies become corrupted. In the narrowness of his self-concern, he is breathing poisoned air. What might have been a great devotion shrivels. What might have been his larger life will die.

That is what happened to Saul. One by one, his generous impulses were destroyed. And that process began in connection with a relationship which had been altogether beautiful.

When David first came to him, he had felt toward David not only the instinctive affection of an older man for a winsome younger one, but also a special gratitude. He had begun to be increasingly troubled because of the breach between himself and the prophet Samuel. It had shaken his security. As he brooded upon it, there came upon him moods of deep depression. But when David played to him on his lyre, the music soothed him and the blackness lifted. He was Saul the king again, determined to go his own way, whatever Samuel or any other influence might say.

Saul had also another reason for valuing David. The intermittent fighting which flared up again and again between Israel and the Philistines had been touch and go. Then there appeared in the Philistine army a new champion, named Goliath, of such terrifying size and strength that there was danger of panic among the Israelites when he appeared. He came out with sword and spear and clothed in armor, and dared any man to come and face him. And who did? Incredibly, David. He had no armor, nor sword either. What he did have was so unheard of for such a contest that Goliath roared with contemptuous laughter. It was a sling, and a handful of smooth stones. But against that weapon the ponderous Goliath had no defense. One single stone hurled from David's sling before Goliath could ever come near enough to use his sword struck the giant in his forehead, and he pitched forward to his death; and when the Philistines saw him fall, they fled. David had won the victory; but Saul was king and therefore it was Saul's victory too. All was going well for him. He could feel his increasing power; and power and men's unquestioned recognition of it were beginning to be the thing that gave him heady satisfaction.

When a man becomes concerned with his own importance, he will want applause. Saul was sure that he would have it. Ever since Samuel had anointed him, he had been the symbol of courage and command in Israel. No wonder the people would remember this, now that the Philistines had been defeated. So he listened with satisfaction when the women poured out of all the cities of Israel singing, "Saul has slain his thousands." But that was not all. They were singing something else, "David has slain his ten thousands!"

So they were putting David first! It was David, not Saul, whom they cared most about. Saul was very angry. And the account in the Book of Samuel foreshadows what would happen next, in one sinister phrase: "Saul eyed David from that day on." The old frank affection was changed to a sidelong suspicious watchfulness. David would be regarded now not as a person significant in himself, but in terms of whether his existence helped or hindered Saul.

When once Saul's jealousy had been roused and his pride offended, there began a disintegration in his character—hidden though it was at first—which those who had known him would not have believed could happen. He wanted to get rid of David; and to accomplish his purpose, he let himself follow a twisted and ugly possibility that cropped up now in his imagination. Pretending to honor David with royal favor, he offered him his daughter Michal in marriage—but with a condition. First David must go out in a new assault against the Philistines and bring Saul the evidence of a hundred men whom he had overcome. If David were killed in the process, who could say that Saul had killed him? And if David were disposed of, was a bit of treachery too serious a price for the advantage to be gained?

But the device backfired. David returned unscarred from the risks into which Saul had sent him. Then Saul's obsession that he must prevail led him further along the path on which what had been best within himself was being sacrificed. He had let his affection for David die. Now he would move on to the blind folly of letting another and more precious relationship be destroyed, even the relationship with Jonathan his son. Jonathan loved David, and because of that Saul was infuriated. So Jonathan would not take his side in the clash of interests which had arisen! Well then, Jonathan was his enemy too. "You son of a perverse, rebellious woman," he shouted at him one day, "do I not know that you have chosen the son of Jesse to your own shame . . . ? For as long as the son of Jesse lives upon the earth, neither you nor your kingdom shall be established!" In his passion he hurled his spear at Jonathan—as he had hurled it at David a short while before to pin him to the wall; and when the spear missed, Jonathan rose and went out from his father's presence "in fierce anger."

It is a long sad story that unfolds in the Book of Samuel, this story of the gradual disintegration of a soul. In trying to assert his dominance, Saul dealt away what ought to have been most precious in his life. He had let personal devotion perish rather than forgo his pride. Alienated from what he once had loved, the last months of his life were a torment of increasing loneliness, the awful loneliness of one who had estranged himself from God in estranging himself from men. In desperation he goes at last to a medium, "the witch of Endor," and begs her to summon up Samuel from the dead; and when the spirit of Samuel appears and demands "Why have you disturbed me by bringing me up?" Saul cries out, "I am in great distress. . . . God has turned away from me and answers me no more!" And the ultimate unraveling of his manhood was revealed in the ignominious self-pity with which one day he accused his servants of having conspired against him and of not being sorry for him, and laid on others the blame for the emptiness which was all that was left for his mind and soul. Therefore, what he would do at the end on the battlefield of Mount Gilboa was not strange. When he took his own sword and fell upon it, he was only symbolizing in one final act the tragedy which he had made of his whole life.

III

Saul, as we have said already, was not alone, either in history or in contemporary life. Other men, like Saul, have been caught in an obsession for power or pre-eminence, and in the end have paid for it at heavy cost.

Herod, king of Judaea when the Romans had conquered Palestine, was called Herod the Great. Such he appeared to be when his skill and ability had pushed his way past rivals to a place of power. It has been written of him that "His courage was high, his understanding capable of large conceptions, and his will able to adhere persistently to a distant end of action." Those "large conceptions" included noble public structures with which he adorned many cities of his kingdom; and, above all, the rebuilding of the Temple in Jerusalem on a scale of magnificence never imagined before. In that respect he appeared to be advancing religion; but in everything he did he was concerned always and altogether with advancing Herod. When he thought his power was endangered he could be ruthless, even to the point of putting to death two of his sons and Mariamne, the Queen whom he had loved. According to the Gospel of Matthew, he ordered the killing of all the young boy children in Bethlehem when he heard the rumor that one had been born there by whom all the sort of kingship he represented would be brought to nothing. He went to all lengths to establish himself and his dynasty, but he did neither. He died frustrated and embittered, knowing that whatever might be the empty pomp of his funeral could not hide the mockery of the fact that all who had rendered him their obsequious honors would be glad that he was dead.

Napoleon Bonaparte rose from obscurity to become emperor of France and the master of most of Europe. He had ability so brilliant and so wide-ranging that he might have left a whole era enriched for his having lived. There was a side of him also that was warm and generous. Lord Rosebery, although an Englishman, wrote of him that in his first better years he was "indulgent and affectionate to his family, dutiful to his mother, kind to his early friends."[1] But as his ambition and his will for dominion grew, he "prepared his own destruction by dealing with men as if they were chequers, and moving them about the board according to his own momentary whim, without a thought of their passion or character or traditions; in a word, by ignoring human nature."[2] To advance his interests he divorced Josephine, his wife, the only woman except his mother whom he had deeply loved; and in so doing "he cut his life in half, and threw away the better part of it."[3] His fatal error was in what another great Frenchman, Ferdinand Foch, was to say about him a

[1] Lord Rosebery, *Napoleon: The Last Phase* (New York: Jonathan Cape and Harrison Smith, 1930), p. 268.

[2] *Ibid.,* p. 256.

[3] James Matthew Thompson, *Napoleon Bonaparte* (New York: Oxford University Press, 1952), p. 328.

hundred years after his death: "He forgot that a man cannot be God; that above the individual is the nation, and above mankind the moral law."[4] So in the end he had forfeited his human friendships. Most of those who had been closest to him deserted him after Waterloo, some with insults; and he died on the stark island of St. Helena, stripped of his greatness, and alone.

It is possible to follow the career of Saul, or of some other great figure who has been like him, as we might follow some tense drama on a stage; and then when the spell of its immediate interest is broken, go on our way with no sense of being involved in that which we have seen. "There is nothing histrionic in my life and character," we may think; "no actuality in me which can be compared with the man of conspicuous possibilities for service who misused them and so fell upon his own sword." But the real drama of a life does not depend upon stage scenery. It does not need to have a highly painted background for its spiritual reality to be significant. Everywhere, and in many men, the essential story of Saul, with its opportunities and the fateful error that may destroy them, can be re-enacted.

Here, for example, is the man in whose hand is the power that comes from political office, or from some other post of special influence in community affairs. What will he do with it, and what loyalty will he chiefly serve? Nobody has visibly anointed him, as Samuel anointed Saul; but his own idealism may anoint him with responsibility, and with recognition of what might otherwise be forgotten, that "above the individual is the nation, and above mankind the moral law." Such a man can become the leader who will lift the thought and will of a whole people to a higher level. But if, on the other hand, he uses his talents only to satisfy his personal ambition, to get promotion no matter what it costs and how many larger values he tramples on the way, he may win the rewards that seem to him success. But he will have destroyed what might have been generous and great-souled in himself; and in the end, though he may not find himself in outward aspects—as Cardial Wolsey said he found himself—"naked to mine enemies," he will find himself naked to that which can have a deadlier thrust, his own conscience which he has made into his foe.

Or suppose a man is trained in medicine. If he has a compassionate heart and an instinctive sympathy for all suffering, he can be—as the Apostle Paul says that Luke was—"the beloved physi-

---

[4] *Ibid.*, p. 439.

cian." He can carry on today the beautiful relationship which was so familiar in an earlier and simpler time, when the family doctor was the friend for whom a whole community was most grateful. But if he becomes concerned most for his convenient office hours, for the fees he can charge and the reputation he can gain beyond the reputation of some rival, then he too has turned the sword destructively against his profession and himself.

And the Church—is that exempt from the failure of Saul? Look and see. Religious conviction and commitment, whether of the ordained minister or the layman, can be of course God's saving power for a world in need. But when instead there is arrogance, and a pride of opinion which pretends to be divine authority, then religion itself has become a perverted weapon.

All those comparisons are true. But beyond them there must be an awareness which comes closer home. It is not in this or that profession or public activity that the tragedy of Saul may be most grievously repeated. It is in those relationships which are most intimate and ought to be most dear. In the home, and not outside it, may be the failure which strikes the deepest wound.

A man loves his wife and children, and he means to love them truly. But being part of human nature and its ancient sins, he also loves himself. And his peril is that he may love too much that part of life which feeds his egotism. He wants to be a person of consequence, and to be recognized as such. Therefore his active imagination and his predominant energies are turned toward those involvements which contribute most to what his pride considers to be success. He is most pleased with those who value what he values. He assumes that his sons ought to admire him and to follow what he wants them to do and to be as they grow up. He does not take time to find out what they actually have in their minds and hearts, or to understand them sensitively. The same may be true even with his wife. Isn't it right that she should approve his pattern, think that his success outside the home is the best asset for all the family, and give him her applause? Like Saul, he may be treating others not always as persons precious in themselves, but as playing their proper parts in an ensemble which centers in him. So the modern Saul, like the ancient one, may wound, if not destroy, the heart of all his life.

Meanwhile the pity of it is that such a man has always had his better nature that might have prevailed. In Saul of the Old Testament the warm heart and the sensitive conscience which once had so conspicuously belonged to him were never quite covered over. Those who had loved him recognized his deeper self and loved him still. Jonathan, who once had left him in fierce anger, stood by his side at the last. David would never lift a hand against him. Almost up to the end Saul might have been saved from his loneliness and his ultimate catastrophe if only he had followed through on what in sudden emotion he cried one day to David: "I have done wrong. I have played the fool, and have erred exceedingly!" May God in his mercy wake that confession, and create a new heart before it is too late, in any of us, the modern Sauls, who have forgotten that self-assertion is a sword that can be turned against one's soul!

5.

Where the Accusing Finger Points

You are the man.
II Samuel 12:7
I have found you.
I Kings 21:20

Not someone else, but you. Not someone else, but we ourselves. The thrust of responsibility and the pointing finger of conscience cannot always be evaded. There are moments when some inescapable moral judgment comes and stands before us and says, "*You* are the man."

Plenty of people will recognize in general that all is not well with the world. The number of persons arrested in the United States for criminal acts has been growing each year, and with a percentage of increase outstripping the growth in population. Worse than that is the fact that crime and delinquency are increasing fastest among half-grown boys and girls; vandalism, house-breaking, stealing of automobiles for crazy joy-rides. And back of the crimes are the ugly causes: poverty and ignorance, unemployment, slum crowding, the break-up of families by desertion and divorce. Add to these things racial conflicts and riots, and there is ironic truth in the reply which a schoolteacher in geography class got one day when she asked her pupils, "What is the shape of the earth?" "My father," volunteered one small boy, "says the earth is in the worst shape it has ever been in. He says, 'It is a mess.'"

We are inclined to agree with that, but we like to assume that it is no fault of ours. "The times are out of joint," we say; and we relieve our feelings by blaming somebody else. "The politicians have been stupid. There have been too many laws—or not laws enough." So we find large, round phrases for explanations of the admitted evils which have come upon us. We are not so ready to admit that the great evils may have grown from our small ones, and that the world-wide ills may have their roots right where we are.

But it is not a good thing to deal in generalities. Truth comes closer home, and it is to the voice of the nearer truth that we need to listen. The words of a spokesman for God which echo from the Bible may be speaking to you and me, "You are the man."

I

Let us remember the circumstances under which those words first were spoken. They belong to one of the most vivid incidents of the Old Testament. It is not a pleasant story. It is told with that unvarnished plainness by which the Old Testament records are always marked; but it has the imperishable dignity of the truth.

David, king of Israel, was in Jerusalem. In this man's character, as we know from his whole story, there were royal qualities of strength and magnanimity, but there were dangerous passions too. One evening David walked on the balcony of his house, and from that balcony his eye fell upon a woman bathing in a garden, and the woman was beautiful. The words which were to be spoken long afterward in the Sermon on the Mount describe the beginning of what happened. "Every one who looks at a woman lustfully has already committed adultery with her in his heart." The fires flared in David's heart that day, and he did not stifle them. Instead he found out who this woman was, and went to her. Her name was Bath-sheba, and her husband Uriah was a soldier in David's own army, then engaged in a campaign against the enemies of Israel. David sent for Uriah, and this man came back from the army to report to the king— a man, as the story shows, of singular courage and devotion. He did not know what was happening at home, and he never knew. For this was what David did. He sent a sealed letter by Uriah's own hand to Joab, the commander of the army, with instructions to Joab that Uriah should be put in the forefront of the next battle, deliberately isolated, and left there to certain death at the enemies' hands. Joab carried out these orders; Uriah was killed; and David took Bath-sheba for his wife.

Baldly recounted thus, the whole action of David seems as cruel, gross, and inexcusable as any human conduct well could be; yet there is no evidence that it appeared so at first to David.

What was happening in his mind and heart? By what influences did it become possible for him to follow such a course as this, apparently without compunction?

To begin with, there was the unreckoning impetuosity of his passion. He had seen something which he desired, and his imagination began to flame in its direction. Modern psychologists have given us new names for old facts, but the facts themselves are as old as life. All his instinctive desires surged into expression. The decent inhibitions which reason and conscience ordinarily would have exercised were removed. The man surrendered to the impulse of the jungle. There was something which he wanted, and he would have it at all costs.

But, of course, David's own idea of the matter was not as crude as this. There were other considerations by which he could rationalize his passions. He was the king. Was it not fitting that the king should have a power denied to ordinary men? Why should he be in a superior position if he could not have superior rights? The arrogance of privilege tinged his thought. It was only as it should be that he should do as it pleased him. If it were not wholly true that the king could do no wrong, nevertheless the king had power which made it possible to argue that any pressing of the question now of right and wrong was only an impertinence.

Furthermore, it may well be that David salved his conscience with the representation to himself in whatever language his time used that between him and Bath-sheba there was what our modern language calls affinity. Who was Bath-sheba's husband? "An ordinary soldier," probably said David to himself, "a rough and common sort of person. And here, on the contrary, am I, elegant and privileged. By all appropriateness, Bath-sheba belongs to me. It will be better for Bath-sheba. That she does not know it, and that Uriah does not know it, is a temporary obstacle, but it can be removed. My business is to take care of my own self-expression, and what I am moved to think is hers."

Thus, very possibly, David reasoned. Or thus, to speak more accurately, he followed his unreasoning urge and clothed its stark fact with the subtle garment of his rationalizing.

Yet his conscience, though hidden, was not destroyed. Under the fierce light of his immediate passion, conscience was blinded, so that for the moment it seemed neither to see nor to estimate his own iniquity. But when he looked at truth objectively, he still saw as well as ever the difference between right and wrong, and presently he was to see the meaning of his own act disclosed in startling fact.

David's sin was personal, but it was not private. No sin ever ultimately is. He thought he could deal with it himself, manage his own responsibilities, and dare the world to interfere. But he could not put a fence around this matter. He had invaded the eternal facts of all morality, and the moral authority of God himself rose up to challenge him. In Jerusalem there was a man whose heart was sensitive to the meanings of God, and this man, Nathan, like all true prophets, had intrepid courage when moral values were at stake. Alone, and clothed only with the power which a fearless conscience gives, he came to David's palace to confront the king.

Also, his wisdom was no less conspicuous than his courage. He did not begin, as a less able man might have done, with blunt condemnation. He had a more crushing end in view. He would make David condemn himself.

Therefore, he began with this story: "There were two men in a certain city, the one rich and the other poor. The rich man had very many flocks and herds; but the poor man had nothing but one little ewe lamb which he had bought. And he brought it up, and it grew up with him and with his children; it used to eat of his morsel, and drink from his cup, and lie in his bosom, and it was like a daughter to him. Now there came a traveler to the rich man, and he was unwilling to take one of his own flock or herd to prepare for the wayfarer who had come to him, but he took the poor man's lamb, and prepared it for the man who had come to him."

Thus under another figure, while David was still unconscious of the fact, the prophet pictured David's own sin. The ruthlessness of the man who, having everything of his own, despoiled the poor man of his lamb, was like the ruthlessness of David, who for his own passion had invaded and destroyed Uriah's home. But David's guard was down, and he was not thinking now of himself. He was absorbed in this stabbing picture which Nathan had brought before him as though for the judgment of the king.

Nathan stopped and waited. Then there happened what he knew would happen. In this picture, so swiftly, so unmistakably drawn, David's higher self—the higher self which was his real self except in the moment of his sins—saw the instant truth. His anger flared into repudiation of this cruelty. "As the Lord lives," he cried, "the man who has done this deserves to die; and he shall restore the lamb fourfold, because he did this thing, and because he had no pity."

Nathan looked at David, and he spoke four words: "You are the man!"

Then he went on with a terrible indictment of this king whom he, the prophet, had been sent, in the name of God, to humble. And at the end he pronounced upon David a judgment which left this powerful and passionate man abject.

But the four words, without those which followed, would have been enough to accomplish his main end. They fell into the inmost citadel of David's soul like high explosive. They dynamited his defenses, set all his conscience on fire, and left him wide open to the full shock of the truth of God which he could not resist. In that fact David represented what in life's circumstances must happen to every human spirit. We may for a while refuse to admit the applicability of moral judgment to our own acts. We may try to treat our own affairs as though they could somehow be hidden from the inescapable realities of God; but sooner or later their truth is projected before us in a form which we cannot fail to recognize. In spite of all the specious veils with which we try to clothe them, our own wrong deeds are seen to be what they are: namely, of one kind with all the mean and dirty and disgraceful things which defile this earth.

Side by side with the act of David, it is well that we should set also another act that is recorded in the Old Testament, for these two belong together in the development of our full thought. In the First Book of Kings there is the story of Ahab and of Naboth. Ahab was king of Israel some century and a half after David. Near his royal palace was a vineyard owned by a man named Naboth, and that vineyard Ahab coveted. He tried to buy it, but Naboth did not want to sell it. It was an inheritance from his fathers, he said, and he could not let it go. But Ahab was sullen with the privileged man's resentment at having his desire crossed. He could not bear to think that his will should be defeated by this common man's resistance. He stopped short of the direct and personal violence which would gain his ends immediately, but he was ready to have someone else pervert justice on his behalf. And the someone else was Jezebel, his wife. She contrived to have Naboth accused on false charges, tried before subservient judges (as Negroes have been accused and tried in white-dominated southern states), condemned and put to death. Now Ahab could be satisfied. Never mind what happened to Naboth.

There was another prophet in Israel then, as indomitable and inescapable as Nathan had been in the time of David. He was Elijah. As Ahab was about to take possession of what he had got from Naboth, there at the gate of Naboth's vineyard stood the man of God. Ahab, caught with his guilty conscience, recoiled. So this prophet had found him out! "Yes, I have found you," Elijah answered, "because you have sold yourself to do what is evil in the sight of the Lord." And he pronounced upon Ahab and all his dynasty the message of judgment and of doom.

Let the two illustrations stand together to illumine the nature of our own possible sins. Both David and Ahab had followed their own desires regardless of the cost. Each had done—or allowed to be done

—a ruthless thing, because they were so much absorbed in themselves that they did not choose to imagine the cruel consequences to those who would be hurt. In the one case, the sin was passion. In the other case, the sin was possessiveness. In one or the other of these the most conspicuous wrongs of our modern life may be rooted. Let us think of them one by one.

II

In the first place, passion.

Is unrestrained passion a sin? our modern age has been asking; and often the answer has been, No. It is not a sin, say some of our pseudo-moralists; it is self-expression; it is the urge of life; it is the casting off of stupid inhibitions to fulfill our personalities.

That is the new phraseology; but it is not a new idea. It is an idea as old as David. Doubtless with such agreeable and satisfactory explanations he interpreted his own act when he seized Bath-sheba and killed Uriah. It was his prerogative as a man of power. Why should he be bound by restraints which his privilege could override? He knew what he wanted, and he would have it. Otherwise, why be king?

That is what he may have said to himself at first, but that is not what he was saying at last when Nathan had confronted him. He knew then that all his real kingliness had been discredited. Before the impact of the moral judgment which overtook him, he stood self-condemned and without excuse. It was a cruel and villainous act which had tied him to the body of all the degradation which dishonors human life. His imagination had been stabbed into awareness. He had begun now to see the situation, not from his own side only, but also from its other side. His supposed satisfaction stood before him, dripping with the blood of its human cost.

The phraseology of much of our present-day teaching in regard to passion—and by passion I mean now, as in the case of David, the passion which has to do particularly with sex—lies in the fact that it narrows the range of consideration so that it does not take in the whole circle of truth. It cultivates a kind of self-absorption which makes all moral judgment grow rancid. Young people are encouraged to think that what they impulsively want is what they have a right to take. Their own small ego, sometimes in its very smallest and meanest aspect, is made commanding. Therefore, they think they can gather the fruits of life in any way which happens to be most easy and irresponsible. They can get physical satisfactions without moral loyalties. They can have their swift taste of pleasure without permanent commitments. If and when they are married, they take this thinly concealed restlessness into marriage also; if their own husband or wife does not satisfy, there is always the expedient of divorce, and somebody else's wife or husband may imaginably prove more desirable.

Once started along this road of self-concern, human beings move like horses with blinders, with no concern for the values they may trample on the way. They do not discipline themselves with any moral scrutiny. They have settled all that by their first assumption that the new morality is to do as they please. Only in some hour of disillusionment, or in some shock of events which produces its own moral awakening, do they begin to see, as David saw, the real meaning of acts which they have sleekly justified, and see themselves arraigned in guilt and shame.

What we need in our age is a new release of understanding. We have had enough of the moral perversion which puts falsehood for truth and tries to make ignoble things seem normal. Surely as we look abroad and perceive in our world the disintegration of many things which have been most beautiful, see the slackening of marriage ties, the cynical prevalence of divorce, the disillusionment of hopes that once were lovely, the breaking up of homes, and that most bitter and cruel tragedy of all, the destruction for little children of the security and spiritual strength which a home ought to have represented, we know that something is gravely wrong in our society. And this something which is wrong traces back to each and every one of us who, like David, has been willing, in opinion or in act, to justify the cruelty of a selfish passion and deliberately to be blind to its inevitable social consequence. It is bad enough to be a part of society in which disrupting influences go on, but what would it be, at some moment of awakening, to look at the human tragedy of love betrayed and ideals violated and to know that we ourselves, by false opinion or by reckless choice, had helped to produce these things, and to hear the voice of an inescapable condemnation saying, "You are the man"?

When in our day people, and especially young people, begin to think that life does not need self-discipline, and that in the matter of their emotions any strong impulse is permissible, it could well be wished that they would go and read those chapters in Charles Dickens' *David Copperfield* which tell of the old house by the sea that Mr. Peggotty had made into a haven of happiness, and where the one most precious to him was the girl he had adopted, who in her lovely innocence was to him like "the one ewe lamb" in Nathan's parable. She was to marry the young fisherman, Ham Peggotty; but Steerforth, the "gentleman," elegant and beguiling, betrayed her guilelessness, and carried her away. And this is the way Dickens describes Ham

Peggotty in an awful moment when the whole tragedy crashed upon him: "The face he turned up to the troubled sky, the quivering of his clasped hands, the agony of his figure, remain associated with that lonely waste in my remembrance to this hour. It is always night there, and he is the only object in the scene."

That is the sort of literary pathos that smacks of "Victorian morality"; some may say, No, in its deep essentials it is not Victorian morality, nor the morality that belongs to any particular period; it is the truth which reaches home to human hearts, the truth of life, which as you read it makes all the pure and cleansing fountains of our understanding flow. There are moral infidelities in this world which are forever wrong, and the end of which is forever tragic. There are some conclusions in these human affairs of ours which are "always night."

Do you remember those words which George Bernard Shaw has put into the mouth of the little priest, De Stogumber? It is in the epilogue of *Saint Joan,* long after Joan was burned, when those who had accomplished her burning, now themselves dead, are revealed again as though they were alive. "I am not cruel by nature, you know," says De Stogumber, and a soldier asks, "Who said you were?" "Well, you see," De Stogumber replies, "I did a very cruel thing once because I did not know what cruelty was like. I had not seen it, you know. That is the great thing: you must see it. And then you are redeemed and saved." Then Cauchon, who had been Bishop of Beauvais, asks, "Were not the sufferings of our Lord Christ enough for you?" And De Stogumber replies that, no, they were not enough; he had to *see* what cruelty is before he could understand. And Cauchon says: "Must then a Christ perish in torment in every age to save those that have no imagination?"[1]

We need to listen to the echo of that question in our modern world. Wherever purity is forgotten, wherever ideals of honor are ignored, wherever passion follows a reckless way, there the purpose of Christ for human life again is being crucified; and it will go on being crucified until you and I and all of us are saved into a new imagination.

III

We have spoken thus far of the sin that grows from passion. We go on finally to speak of the sin that grows from possessiveness. Of this, not David, but Ahab was the exemplar.

Passion has to do with persons. Possessiveness may more often

[1] (New York: Brentano's, 1924), p. 154.

have to do with things, and this time in which we live has been a time in great measure obsessed with things. This civilization of the Western world is, as Tawney the English economist has suggestively called it, "our acquisitive society"; and in this acquisitive society, which all of us in some measure shape, there can be cruelties not greatly different from the cruelty of Ahab when in his preoccupation with what he wanted he had no concern for what his gain might be costing someone else.

We profess as our belief that every human being is equally entitled to life, liberty and the pursuit of happiness. But what are some of the actual facts? Tens of thousands of the underprivileged have no largeness of life, little happiness, and no freedom to defend themselves against the powerful. In the rat-ridden slums of American cities the children of the poor have a disease rate and a death rate in tragic contrast to the well-being of the children on the avenue, because rapacious landlords can make money out of rotten tenements while the community does not care. In rural districts sharecroppers may be ordered off the land they have worked and out of the shacks which are all that they have had to live in if they ask for decent wages. A sick or injured Negro may be turned away from a hospital because he is not white. And men and women who have dared to challenge racial injustice and oppression—as in Alabama and Mississippi—have been murdered in cold blood, and courts have let the murderers go free.

"But what has all that to do directly with me?" some one of us may ask. "I have not done any of those things." No, but we have let them be done by somebody else while we made no protest, and have gone on enjoying our satisfactions while others suffered. Ahab did not go out and seize Naboth's vineyard himself, but he let Jezebel go out and get it for him. And many of us who belong to the privileged classes have let social iniquities continue as long as we were comfortable, and have tried to tell our consciences that we were not responsible.

But often in a deep sense we are responsible, if the safeguarding of our own interests has kept our thought and sympathy and our determination from being aroused. It has been truly said that the greatest tragedy of this period of social transition could be "not the strident clamor of the bad people, but the appalling silence of the good people. Our generation will have to repent not only for the acts and words of the children of darkness but also for the fears and apathy of the children of light."[2]

[2] Martin Luther King, Jr., *Stride Toward Freedom* (New York: Harper & Row, 1958), p. 202.

The best in us could be aroused if we should look at the whole of life and not—as Ahab did—only at our selfish advantage in it. A thoughtful research psychiatrist who has spent "the past five years studying Negro and white families caught up in the various crises of desegregation in the cities of both the south and the north" describes one Negro family, made up of a mother and three sons. Of the two older sons, one has become a heavy drinker, uninterested in work; the second a resentful, aloof man who mistreats his wife and children, gambles heavily, and has been several times arrested for stealing. The youngest son had the chance to get into a good school, which had been desegregated, was graduated with honors, and liked by his white classmates, "almost in spite of ourselves," as one of them put it. And this is what the mother said of the three:

They say we're lazy and we don't pay much attention to the law, and sure enough I have two boys to prove it and one to disprove it, so it's two to one against us in this family. But I'd like to tell people why I think my two boys went bad.

I preached and hollered at all three the same. Those older boys were good boys just like the little one, and I remember when they wanted to study and be somebody, just like him. But they never had a chance. They were born too soon. That was it.

They went to school until it didn't make any sense to stay there, because we had no money and they thought they should try to get jobs. So they left school and tried. They tried and tried and there wasn't anything for them.

I wonder, do people who never have to worry about work know what happens to you when you keep on knocking your head on a stone wall and there's still no work? I'll tell you what, your head bleeds, and you get tired; you get so tired that you give up. You just fold up and die.

I watched my boys go bad like milk you know is standing too long there's no use for it, so it get sour. All those people out there, do they ever see how we live and what we have to take all the time? My boys, they were once good, and they wanted so bad to get jobs, and make something of themselves.[3]

"They wanted so bad to . . . make something of themselves"! *There* is the pitiableness of lives from whom society has taken away what they might have had, as Ahab took away the inheritance of Naboth. Who is responsible for that injustice? Not only the world in general. To some of us, so content with our own possessions and our privilege that we have no outgoing sympathy, there may come the prophet's answer, "*You* are the man."

[3] Robert Coles, in the *Washington Post,* Oct. 10, 1965.

6.

What the Great Responsibility Can Create

Should such a man as I flee?
NEHEMIAH 6:11

HERE IS a man who was being advised to scuttle his responsibility and hide himself or else be killed; and here was his indignant answer. Somebody else in the same circumstances perhaps might cut and run, but not he. "I am not that kind of a man."

What any man will do in a crisis depends upon his own instinctive estimate of what he is and what he means to be. If he thinks meanly of himself, what he does will be ignominious. If he has a noble self-awareness, then he will be incapable of meanness. The old proverb is often quoted, "Pride goeth before a fall"; but there is a sort of pride which is the strongest assurance that a man will not fall. False pride—the pride which is a pompous attempt to cover up self-conscious pettiness, the puffed-up pride of vanity and self-importance—is contemptible. But there is a saving pride which comes from inner integrity, and because of it there can be a strength of character which revolts from any unworthy and degrading thing. It is the presence of *that* pride which makes a man's goodness dependable.

The extraordinary fact about the Bible is that although its dates go a long way back, the people in it could all be contemporary. The setting of their stage is different, but the drama of their spiritual destinies resembles ours. Their problems are like our problems, their duties like our duties, and from their efforts and achievements there can come a stimulus to quicken ours.

The particular person who spoke the words, "Should such a man as I flee?" was the central figure in the ancient Book of Nehemiah. Not many people are named Nehemiah today (though in the Puritan era in New England when everybody was familiar with the Old

Testament many men were); and no one finds himself in exactly the circumstances which Nehemiah faced. But everyone, whether yesterday, today or tomorrow, would be the better off for having the sort of integrity which Nehemiah had—and for knowing how to gain and keep it.

Therefore let us look at history and remember the facts about him.

When the story of his life begins, he was in a position which certainly did not give any special promise that a career of distinction lay ahead. A century and a half earlier Jerusalem and all Judaea had been conquered by the Babylonians, and many of the Jewish people carried captive into the east. It was from these captives that Nehemiah was descended. Conditions in the captivity had not been too harsh; and after the Persians broke the power of Babylon, not harsh at all. Now Nehemiah was in Susa, the Persian capital; and he was a sort of minor official in the court of the Persian king.

He could have stayed there comfortably enough, but there was something that disturbed him. He learned that new disasters had come upon Jerusalem and upon the Jewish remnant who had tried to establish life there again. "That is bad, but what can I do about it?" he might have said. As a matter of fact, what he did say to himself was very different; and the whole Book of Nehemiah is the story of what he did, and of the manner of man he became. What he became would be revealed in the question he was to ask, "Should such a man as I flee?" and the forces which made him able to arrive at that point of his developed manhood were two.

In the first place, the fact that he was committed to a loyalty big enough to demand his best;

And second, the fact that he was able to meet increasing tests by the way in which he had met other tests before.

I

He might not have been committed to anything at all except his own advantage. He could stay in the court of the Persian king, where he was held in favor. But he took what he had heard about Jerusalem on his conscience. Jerusalem had been the center of Jewish life. It was more than a place where a certain number of individuals might have their habitations. It was the symbol of a people's soul. While Jerusalem was standing, men could believe in the continuing covenant which God had given to the faith of Abraham, and which had been the central flame in Jewish history since Abraham's time. Every great hope also for the future was bound up with what might happen to Jerusalem, and especially with the expectation which the prophet Isaiah had proclaimed.

> It shall come to pass in the latter days
>   that the mountain of the house of the Lord
> shall be established as the highest of the mountains,
>   and shall be raised above the hills;
> and all the nations shall flow to it,
>   and many peoples shall come, and say:
> "Come, let us go up to the mountain of the Lord,
>   to the house of the God of Jacob,
> that he may teach us his ways
>   and that we may walk in his paths."
> For out of Zion shall go forth the law
>   and the word of the Lord from Jerusalem.

That was the sort of imagination which moved Nehemiah. To him, Jerusalem was not only a place; it was a principle. It was meant to be the Holy City. It could be a witness to the purpose of God in the midst of human life. To help to rebuild it therefore could give a new dimension to a man's existence. It could involve him in something so significant that calculations of his own advantage, fears for his own safety, temptations to slide out from under the load if it should seem too heavy, could be forgotten.

Having been gripped by a great purpose, Nehemiah could not rest until he had done something to advance it. The first thing he did was to go to Artaxerxes the Persian king, and ask for permission to go to Jerusalem to see what the facts might be. He did get permission, and he went. As to the facts, they were bad enough. What had been the walls of Jerusalem were nothing but a heap of broken stones. The people were bewildered and discouraged. They needed a conception of something great to work for; and in the strength of that, the will to work. Nehemiah brought them both. "The God of heaven will make us prosper," he said, "and we his servants will arise and build."

Is there anything that has to be remote from us in what Nehemiah represented? On the contrary, every life that would have any nobility in it must express the double fact which Nehemiah's life embodied: a vision, and the everyday faithfulness which can turn it into fact.

When we speak of vision, let us not suppose that we mean something mystical and remote, outside the ken of the average human being. What we do mean is the light to guide him which every man can have when he keeps his thought and imagination directed to the best he knows. Then like Nehemiah, he will realize one day that he can help "rebuild Jerusalem": help—that is to say—to create in the midst of life an influence which transmits the spirit of God. If in his heart a man really wants to do that, he will be doing it, even when he does not know how real his contribution is. In the Book of Nehemiah (open the Old Testament and read it) there is one long chapter which seems completely dull. It is nothing but a list of individuals and of families who worked on the walls of Jerusalem, and where they worked; and some of the work was at inconspicuous places, with no glamour in it. But the point is that *every* part of the work was important, because if any of it had been neglected the walls would have been incomplete; and every part that *was* well done made possible the new Jerusalem which could be a shrine of the presence of God.

If that was true in Nehemiah's time, it is equally true now. "The work," said Nehemiah, "is great and widely spread." Most of the work that any one of us is called upon to do may be involved in what seems ordinary, everyday affairs. The Holy City is not built only by what men do on Sundays. It is built by what we severally do, beginning Monday, out at our several posts—in the office, in the shop, in our housekeeping, in our responsibility for common things. By what we accomplish there and then we help—or do not help—to create the Holy City.

There is no such thing as merely "secular" work, in the disparaging meaning of that word, if the work we are engaged in is touched with a consecrating purpose. In any honest and legitimate business, in any helpful post of service whatever, it is possible in the deepest sense to glorify God. It is not so much great sermons that the world needs as steady faithfulness in all its familiar work. It is well that we should realize this as deeply and richly as we can, in estimating our own life and the lives of others. In *The Autobiography of Henry M. Stanley*[1] there is a passage which reveals with fine simplicity how a lofty spirit can treat obscure responsibilities in such a way as to make their meaning great. It was when this man—who ultimately was to explore untraveled Africa, unlock the secrets of the continent's dark heart, and find the lost David Livingstone—was a boy who had drifted friendless into a city which he had never seen before. He found for himself work in a grocery store, and this is what he wrote of his days there: "I own to be proud that I had no fear of soiling my hands or my clothes with work, and I never allowed a leaky sack of coffee, or barrel of flour to leave our store for want of a little sewing or cooper-

[1] (Boston and New York: Houghton Mifflin Co., 1909), p. 94.

ing—tasks which the other clerks felt it beneath them to do." Good right did he have to be proud, and good right has every single life to be proud that by thoroughness and high faithfulness it puts into common tasks that quality of high integrity which is building up—whether it knows it or not—the walls of a finer trust for all humanity in the principles which are of God.

There is an inspiring letter too in the *Life of Octavia Hill,* the great-souled Englishwoman of the nineteenth century who did perhaps as much as anyone of her generation to change the wretched conditions under which the poor of London lived; and who, out of the seemingly prosaic details of buying miserable tenements and making them decent and sweet for human habitation, created a fellowship of human service into which she drew some of the noblest spirits of her time. She wrote to a friend of hers who was restless and disheartened because he imagined that his life could not count for much in the uninspiring business he had had to enter:

When work is good in its object, as merchant's work must be, is it not pretty sure that a good man, whose path has led him straight into the thick of it, seeing its abuses and its temptations, has a distinct calling? The difficulties are the foundation of the triumph. The world is all full of them. We grope about, and seem hardly to see our way; but if honestly, moment by moment, we do as much as we see, somehow the place is better for our presence; and in the long years, looking back, we feel that we have been led on by paths we did not see, towards ends we hardly dreamed of reaching.[2]

I think of a trained nurse about whom no public record may be written, but for whom many in the city where she lives have continual reason to be grateful. She represents to an extraordinary degree the dedication which can turn what might be only making a living into a vital contribution to many people's lives. Others in her profession will do what they are expected to do, but she never stops at that. In the strain of nursing some desperately ill person, there may be days when she is half ill herself, but no one will know it. With steady courage and cheerfulness she keeps on. In mind and heart she gives to her patient a quick imagination for the extra helpfulness that goes beyond all routine. And in being what she is, she has created for many people, in their times of suffering, strongholds of inner trust and peace because they have been defended by a human goodness through which there shines a spirit that could have come only from God.

So the truth widens out into its relationship with all of us: the

---

[2] C. Edmund Maurice (London: Macmillan and Co., 1913), p. 508.

truth that a spiritual value may be brought into our present world even when we are unaware—as those whom Nehemiah inspired may have been unaware—of the ultimate significance of what we do. Here are men who, with a desire deeper than they themselves quite know or can express, want to contribute something that will count for nobleness in their place and time. They know that they may never be set apart for the kind of work which they consider distinctively religious. They will never preach or ever be bound up officially with any ecclesiastical or philanthropic agency. They must work hard for a living in the midst of a business competition the pressure of which is unrelenting. They must be immersed every day in what seem to be material details. And here are women who are shut within the circle of necessities narrower still. They must spend the best of their strength in the petty cares of the household, trying to make meager incomes cover growing expenses, working, planning, spending themselves unreservedly as it seems for the needs of the others for whom they must make the home a happy place. Well, what shall these men and women think of themselves? Shall they imagine that their duties have no lofty worth? Shall they think as men in Jerusalem long ago might have thought who should have looked at the monotonous business of laying the uninspiring stones into their small section of the wall and said to themselves that it was all too poor a concern for their hearts to kindle to? Or shall they rather see—as those men in Jerusalem did see—the greatness of their opportunity? For great it is, even though so obscure. To take a church, as a sexton does, and keep it clean, to tend its furnaces and open its doors, is a work that a man may be proud of if he has done it well. To take pride in doing better work than necessity calls for or than men expect; to take a business that small souls would make common and to carry into it an ideal that makes its conduct uncommon; to take an office or a profession that might be used for private profit and to ennoble it with the spirit of public service; to use an industrial or financial crisis not as a chance to make a shrewd and selfish gain but as an opportunity to serve the people's need; to carry into all work the ideals of so high an integrity that all who are associated in it are made the better for their daily duties—this is to render both to man and to God supreme service, and to create the spiritual bulwarks behind which all good living can be secure.

II

Thus far, then, we have considered the first of the two influences which made Nehemiah the kind of man whose integrity could not be shaken: the fact that he was committed to a loyalty big enough to demand his best. We go on to consider the second truth about him: the fact that he was able to meet increasing tests because of the way he had met other tests before.

The record begins with the moment when he heard of the desperate situation in Jerusalem. There was need for someone who would set out to help; but he might jeopardize his own safety if he dared to ask that he be allowed to go and do it. Who could tell whether the Persian king might not be suspicious and resentful if any subject of his volunteered to try to rebuild the defenses of a conquered city which had often been troublesome? Why not wait to see how the winds might blow?

Nehemiah admits that he was "very much afraid." But if he was, he did not yield to his timidity. He told the king the truth about his desire. No matter how he felt inside, he followed what his conscience told him, and he got permission to go to Jerusalem. That was the first step on the way ahead.

Next came his arrival at the ruined city. He rode around the rubble, which was all that was left of the walls—at night and alone, so that he would not be observed. He had heard in Persia a report of how bad the conditions were, but to see them directly now was something else, and worse. Also he realized that he was not the first who had confronted what looked like an appalling venture. A company of exiles who had been allowed to come back from Persia at an earlier time had tried to restore the city, and had failed. What likelihood was there that any new effort could be successful? If he had had to overcome timidity before, now he had to face discouragement. But the best way to face it was to outface it, and that was what he did. "You see the trouble we are in," he said to the people whom he gathered round him. Then what? Then, nevertheless, "Let us rise up and build."

So they did begin to build; but a third and subtler test confronted Nehemiah. Three men who were hostile to anything he might try to do, Sanballat, Tobiah and Geshem, an Arab, began to ridicule what had been set on foot. "What are these feeble Jews doing?" they wanted to know. "Will they restore things? Will they finish up in a day? Will they revive the stones out of the heaps of rubbish, and burned ones at that?"

Of all the weapons that can be used against an effort that rises above the ordinary level, ridicule may be the deadliest. People can go along with what seems to be common sense, but they may begin to flinch when some loud objector derides them as being credulous and silly. Or when he represents what they try to do as being only a parade of piousness. That could happen a long time ago, and it can happen now. Let a man in any modern community who is ahead of his time champion some program of social justice and of broad human welfare which runs counter to selfish interests. Let a man in the Congress of the United States, or in any other governing body, speak for some generous ideal of world-wide understanding and cooperation which rouses the scorn of narrow nationalists and professional "patriots." And what will happen? They cry: "What are these do-gooders up to now? Do they think they can change human nature and make the world over?"

That glib word "do-gooders" is not only shallow and cheap. It contains a hidden blasphemy. In the house of Cornelius at Caesarea, the Apostle Peter preached in the name of one who "went about doing good," and that one was Jesus. Let anyone therefore if he is called a "do-gooder" thank God insofar as he *is* one, and look with pity on the man so twisted as to imply that doing good is something to be ashamed of. Yet there are some who will be put out of countenance by the slurring word, and drop the fine cause they had believed in when it is met with ridicule. That is what Nehemiah did *not* do; and men of brave and steady confidence in the ultimate strength of goodness will not do it now.

One more serious test was waiting for Nehemiah before the final one. It did not come from enemies without. It came from within. One group of those who were supposed to be building the walls were taking advantage of another group, and there was danger that the whole effort might be split apart.

The poorer people who had lived on the land outside the walls of Jerusalem had been brought in for the rebuilding. With no time now to cultivate the ground and grow food, they had fallen into debt to men who had money. Heavy mortgages were on the little that they owned, and meanwhile prices were going up because of the black market controlled by the powerful few. It was the kind of commercial cruelty which has been practiced often before and since.

"But these are private transactions," it might have been said, "and no business of yours, Nehemiah." If that *had* been said, it would have been the same "let us alone" reply which exploiting groups have made in modern times. "Religion and the church, and especially preachers, should attend to their own affairs and not meddle with economic issues. Let them talk about God, but not in disturbing fashion, and especially not with any reference that would rub vested interests on the raw." But for Nehemiah no such conception as that could be listened to. He confronted immediately the men whom he believed to have been guilty of exploitation—and be it said that they met him with a more open-minded and conscionable response than some of their successors have shown. In any case, Nehemiah had not dodged the issue. He knew that righteousness and truth had to be relevant not only to a part of life but to all of it, if there were to be any actual building of a City of God.

So when the final test came the outcome of it had been assured already. He had measured up to his full manhood too many times for there to be any chance that he would fail at the end, even though what confronted him was a threat against his life. A man who had been suborned by Sanballat and Tobiah to be their secret agent told him that he would be assassinated that night unless he fled—and turned the temple into a hiding place. The threat itself was a lie, but Nehemiah did not know that. The likelihood seemed grim enough. It was plain that there were men who would be ready to kill him if they got the chance. Nevertheless, he brushed the threat aside. "Should such a man as I flee? . . . I will not!" He had not fallen into the snare of betraying himself by thinking first of his own safety. And after that there was nothing more that the forces arrayed against him could do. The day came when he could write, "So the wall was finished . . . and there was very great rejoicing."

Thus it was made clear what a man can accomplish when he is possessed by a great purpose, and when by the courage that grows through increasing tests he gains the proved integrity which nothing can at last assail.

7.

The Perishable and the Permanent

> King Nebuchadnezzar . . . was walking on the
> roof of the royal palace of Babylon, and the
> king said, "Is not this great Babylon, which I
> have built by my mighty power as a royal
> residence and for the glory of my majesty?"
>
> DANIEL 4:28

SO THE old words echo down across the centuries, in gorgeous ancient boastfulness which the ironic course of history has mocked! There is much in the Bible about Nebuchadnezzar as king and conqueror, and we know enough about Babylon to understand how evident it seemed that the lord of Babylon had cause to boast. The great city stood astride the Euphrates River, drawing its wealth from the wide richness of the Mesopotamian plains; protected by vast walls and gates from enemies; and within those walls its royal palaces and "the hanging gardens" which were among the wonders of the world. In the seventh and sixth centuries B.C., the Babylonian armies swept westward as far as the Mediterranean coast to conquer Tyre, captured and destroyed Jerusalem, and broke the power of Egypt. The grandeur of Babylon was still proverbial when the Book of Revelation was written, so that it was remembered as "the great city that was clothed in fine linen, in purple and scarlet, bedecked with jewels, and with pearls!"

Nebuchadnezzar reigned for more than forty years, and when he died in 561 B.C. Babylon still seemed to be the symbol of glory and of wide dominion. But in 538, less than a quarter of a century after Nebuchadnezzar's death, the city fell to Cyrus, king of Persia; and the Babylonian empire disappeared from among the powers of the earth. Instead of the pride which Nebuchadnezzar had voiced, there could echo now the terrible taunt which sounds in the fourteenth chapter of the Book of Isaiah.

> How you are fallen from heaven,
> O Day Star, Son of Dawn!

How you are cut down to the ground,
you who laid the nations low! . . .
Sheol beneath is stirred up
to meet you when you come,
it rouses the shades to greet you
all who were leaders of the earth;
it raises from their thrones
all who were kings of the nations.
All of them will speak
and say to you,
"You too have become as weak as we!
You have become like us!"
Your pomp is brought down to Sheol,
the sound of your harps;
maggots are the bed beneath you,
and worms are your covering.

In our time archaeologists dig in what had appeared to be only featureless mounds in the deserts to uncover the fragmentary ruins of what once was Babylon; and there in the emptiness where only the jackals prowl it is as though the voice of the dead centuries were speaking:

The worldly hope men set their hearts upon
Turns Ashes—or it prospers; and anon
Like Snow upon the Desert's Dusty Face,
Lighting a little hour or two—was gone.[1]

Babylon and its destruction were a long time ago, and if Babylon stood alone we might forget it. But it is not alone. Again and again in the long course of history it has been made plain that "the worldly hope men set their hearts upon" may perish. Empires and civilizations which imagined that they were indestructible have gone down to death. Nor is it any defense against calamity for a particular people to think that for itself this cannot be true.

Nebuchadnezzar never dreamed that the glory and majesty he looked upon was about to disappear. Alexander the Great, when he led his Grecian armies across the Hellespont to conquer wide king-doms in Asia, did not know that in a few months he would be dead and that his conquests would die with him. Rome in the time of Augustus Caesar, when its legions were the masters of all the Western world, had no conception that before long the barbarians would be at

---

[1] *The Rubáiyát of Omar Kháyyám*, trans. by Edward Fitzgerald.

the gates. Philip of Spain, when his galleons were bringing back the plundered riches of the Americas, could not see the hand of judgment which was writing, as the moving finger wrote on the walls of Belshazzar's banquet hall, that his empire was at an end. And still closer to our time, and more poignant, is the waning of the imperial power of Great Britain. It was only a few years ago that Winston Churchill declared that he "did not become the King's first minister in order to preside over the dissolution of the British Empire." But under his immediate successors inexorable facts have blotted out great areas of that empire, like the shadow of a long eclipse moving across the sun.

I

Thus it is true that there are human ambitions, and also great actual achievements, which are perishable. Beginning with the dramatic words which had to do with Babylon, we have been thinking of the fate of nations. But a nation is no impersonal entity. It is made up of people, and what a nation is will be what the people are. If a nation is to have a soul, and if the communities within it are to have some meaning bigger than blind agglomerations of material things, then it must all depend upon what the multitudes of men and women like ourselves shall think and choose and do.

One of the immortal parables of Jesus is his parable of the man who wanted to build bigger barns, and then fill them up with more and more brought in from his fields. He had as much as he needed already, but that did not satisfy him. He wanted to lay up so much more that he could be sure he could take his ease, eat, drink, and be merry the rest of his days. Then everything would be provided for. But one thing he had forgotten, and that was his soul. "That night," said the voice of God, "your soul is required of you; and the things you have provided, whose will they be?"

The crucial fault in the man of Jesus' parable was not so much in what he did as in what he was not doing. To cultivate his fields and to make ready to store his crops was in itself a natural thing to do. Without that kind of action the world would go hungry. But in his case, what was it chiefly for? To feed his pride of large possessions, to give him such surplus that for the rest of time he could indulge himself. What he did *not* do was to say, "This is what is happening to things, but what is happening to me?" If he had stopped to ask that, he would have seen that though his material wealth was increasing, he was shriveling. Wrapped up in himself, he had no concern for larger interests. In his obsession for getting more, he was losing any meaning for his life.

There is a Russian legend which is in tune with Jesus' parable—the legend of a peasant who could never be content because he was always hearing of richer lands that could be had in the next province beyond his own. Continually he was selling what he had and going after the bigger chance. At last he reached the province where lay the fattest land of all Russia, and he was told that he could have all the land he could walk around in a day; but that if he failed to finish the boundaries, nothing that he had measured would be his. Out he started then early in the morning, his eyes shining with delight at this fertile soil that was to be his own. Noon came, and still he went straight on. The land was too good for him to stop yet from reaching out to encompass more. It was afternoon when he commenced to alter his course, so that he might bend the boundary and enclose the area of possessions which would be his. The afternoon waned. The shadows began to lengthen. He was a long way from his starting point. On he went with desperate haste, his muscles flagging, the blood beating in his ears. A long way off, he saw the starting point as the sun went down, with a crowd of people watching to see whether he would arrive. He drove himself with one final terrific effort, swayed forward to claim his wide possessions, staggered, and fell down dead.

Men whose minds are hypnotized thus with the possibility of great material gain, who gaze at "this great Babylon which I have built" or hope to build, do not fall down dead with dramatic suddenness. But nevertheless the fact may be that something in them dies. Generous interests atrophy. Ideals of service are pushed aside as too quixotic. There are parents who are concerned not for their children's real growth but that their children may gain all the artificial things which will make them appear successful. There are rich people who would feel a distinct mortification if their sons did not go into some kind of business that would make them opulent too, who would think that the family prestige had been diminished if this boy who might have been a financial magnate goes instead into teaching, or throws his organizing ability into some form of social service which will never give him more than a scanty salary, or offers himself as a missionary in some place where to them his life seems lost. There are mothers who will go to any extreme to see that their daughters meet those whom they consider eligible young men of fortune. But these ambitions also are like the "snow upon the desert's dusty face" which "lighting a little hour or two" is gone.

II

The fallacy which is as old as Babylon, the proud assumption that accumulations of prestige and power can endure, may be repeated thus in individual families. It can be repeated also where it least ought to appear—in that which ideally is the great family of the spirit, the Christian Church.

What are the ways in which too often we reckon the kind of success we think the Church has attained? By so many figures of members on the rolls, by the amount of money given to it, by growing endowments. There may be the perilous tendency to think in terms of size and quantity instead of asking the disturbing question: What quality of life is the Church producing? Some forty years ago, in the heyday of the campaign to gather funds for the building of the great cathedral on Morningside Heights in New York, there was a kind of fascinated recital of its dimensions. It would be so many feet long, so many feet wide, and its towers so many feet high. It would be not only the biggest cathedral in America but, with one or two regrettable exceptions, the biggest in the world. "In bulk, in cubic contents," one fervent if irrelevant orator proclaimed, it would leave nothing but St. Peter's in Rome to outmatch it. And the extent to which the great realities could for the moment be forgotten was exemplified by one gentleman from Wall Street who made a plea so astonishing that those who heard it are not likely to forget it; for his argument was that a great church could help to insure a community against radical ideas, and men of wealth had better pay for their insurance! It would be untrue to say that he was typical; yet there have been and are others who share his belief that the Church should be a reliable bulwark for the social and economic status quo. In 1965 the Bishop of New York discovered that any early completion of the cathedral was being jeopardized by resentment against some particular causes which he had championed. "I have learned," he said, "that a very large gift towards the completion of this great Cathedral was stricken out of one man's will because of the Diocese's stand on Civil Rights. That happened to be in Manhattan. In other parts of the Diocese, this Cathedral which I would like to see completed has lost financial support because of the stands that I as a Bishop of the Church of God have felt compelled to take."

Then he spoke this noble word in which the real soul of the Church found utterance: "If in the providence of God it turns out to be that this unfinished condition is going to prevail for years, then I can only hope that its very unfinished quality will stand as a memorial to a Diocese which in the 20th Century tried to do what it believed was right."

Are figures and statistics and money and the favor of the well-to-do of any ultimate value in the development of souls? The Roman Catholic Church, notwithstanding its curious compromises in many particulars with the spirit of this world, yet has also its inspired insights into the value of those forces which may seem insignificant according to the world's measurements, but are unique in their eternal worth. It has often surrounded the papacy with pagan splendor, but it remembers also the lovely figure of St. Francis, and puts "the little poor man of Assisi" in the roll of her immortals. As against scheming for political power and the regimented formalism of worship which goes on in many of its churches, Rome does have the redeeming fact that now and then it produces great sainthood; and to produce one saint is a greater glory for any church than all the material gains that can be added up in any reckoning. Who that has had any part in the life of Christian congregations does not thank God most for some of the lives which have flowered in them? I think of men who have gone gallantly about their daily business under heavy handicaps of difficulty and of sorrow, ready to forget their own advantage in their love for others or their loyalty to a cause which meant more to them than their own concerns. I think of a person who, so far as the figures on the calendar are concerned, might seem to have left the best of her life behind her. But in her spirit the courage and sweetness of life breathes, like the distillation from all the flowers of a garden. She is not too ethereal for human nature's daily food. She has her likes and dislikes, and her little whimsicalities of expression. But whenever one comes into touch with her, one goes away feeling that life is a sweeter and a braver thing than it might have seemed to be an hour before. In the range of her activities and in the things which she has to do, there is nothing that one can call bigness; but from her, as from a little piece of radium, incalculable spiritual potencies go out. To produce spirits like that is the miracle of religion. Wherever they are, there in them is the real splendor and greatness of our human life.

In the present time there is increasing awareness also of the wider standard by which the Church must be measured. It must not only bring refinement of spirit and transformation to individual lives. It must be a power for righteousness in the whole life of a community and a nation. Some who are entrenched in their selfish privileges and too much blinded by their own interests to see the truth will not acknowledge that. They want the church "to comfort the afflicted" but emphatically not "to afflict the comfortable." So there will be those who—like the men and women who canceled their intended gifts to the Cathedral in New York because the church in controversial issues had championed the disadvantaged and the poor—want the Church to be a sort of satisfied Babylon built all for them. But such a church invites the verdict written long ago by the relentless hand of judgment. "You have been weighed in the balances and found wanting." Any organization of religion that is useless will wither and disappear, and only those aspects of the Church which are linked with justice and mercy and living service can have in them the permanence that belongs to God.

III

It is difficult for any people to believe that what they have built or inherited can be perishable. The appearance of authority and power may be so overweening that any doubt of its continuance may wake an angry scorn. Who wants to hear any voices questioning an enduring dominion for these United States? What other nation has ever had its vast resources; its fertile plains, its forests, and its rivers; its incredible scientific and industrial complex and the genius that created it? Is it not obviously "God's country," lifted up uniquely above such fate as has befallen great empires of the past?

So in complacency we might think. But there are tremors in the ground; tremors that might presage convulsions of this planet so awful as to shake the foundations of everything that was supposed to be enduring. The rise of new nations in Africa and Asia not yet used to freedom and in some cases embittered because of what they may think to have been their long exploitation as colonies of the West, the spread of Communism, the vast menace of alienated China, the shadow of the hydrogen bomb—who can surely see the future through these portentous shapes? And the possible coming of an atomic war, with the cataclysmic ruin which would be the end of that, is not the only peril. If the present drifts continue, the growing apprehension might so destroy faith and hope that this nation also might come under the dominance of the military mind, and the freedoms which have been its glory disappear.

At the time of Queen Victoria's jubilee, when England seemed to stand at the apex of its grandeur, Rudyard Kipling had the illumination which made him write the solemn magnificence of the *Recessional.* Not pride, but the inspired power of prophecy that seized him and went perhaps beyond his own intention, was throbbing in its lines. Already the great symbols of possibilities which he foresaw are beginning to turn into fact. After the two world wars which few in Kipling's time could have believed would come, it is true for the military might and the material power of England that "on dune and headland sinks the fire." Who can dare to say for any nation, including ours, that the day may not come when

> Lo, all our pomp of yesterday
> Is one with Nineveh and Tyre!

Our pomp of yesterday: suppose the pomp did go. Would that be the end of the story? No, it would not! For pomp and power are not what are of ultimate weight in the balances of God. The tragedy of many of the great empires of antiquity was that physical power, and often brutal power, was all that they did have. No great light for mind and spirit was kindled by Assyria or Babylon, by Attila or Tamerlane. But some nations *have* created a heritage by which all the world is permanently enriched. The little kingdom in Judaea that produced the prophets did. Greece of Socrates and Plato and Phidias and Praxiteles and her dramatists did. And in our present century if it should prove that Great Britain will not again wield the dominion which once it held, its greatness will neverthe- less be immortal: the greatness of having developed the institutions under which men can grow in freedom, and of having defended them with a courage which the world has looked upon with awe. There are triumphs of the spirit which neither time nor change can dim; and the heroic fortitude of England when it stood undaunted through two world wars has given to mankind a heritage which another thousand years of empire could not surpass.

IV

Then there is a final fact which is the climax of our thinking, and of our hope. It may be that the peoples of the earth have reached a point in history when old evil obsessions begin to lose their enslaving power. For countless centuries the tribes and then the nations have assumed that the advantage, and sometimes the actual existence, of any one depended on what it could take away from others. So came the endless wars of attempted conquest and spoliation, with no sense of a destiny for the whole of humanity in which all men must inevitably be involved. But in this century there have come a development of communication hitherto unimaginable, by which men anywhere can know what is happening everywhere; a new sense that whatever of good or of evil appears in any place will have its reverberations around the world; and a realization that all the peoples on this shrunken planet have got to learn to live together, or else go down in indiscriminate and perhaps universal doom and death.

In the United States in 1965 there was launched what was called the program for the Great Society. Its immediate reference was and is domestic. That is to say, it represents an effort to mobilize the resources and energies of the nation for the aid of those within its own boundaries who need aid most. It is built upon the recognition that there cannot be ignorance and poverty and deprivation and despair in any group without the life of all the people being somehow degraded. So a large part of the public funds—drawn as a matter of fact mostly from the taxes paid by the prosperous— is to be used to raise the level of existence where it is most depressed; to eliminate filthy slums, to save some open spaces where the children of the poor can play, to build better schools and train better teachers, to make the cities not breeding-grounds for increasing crime but areas of hope where every child may have a decent chance to develop the best that is in him. In any human enterprise there is the imperfection of mixed motives. In this pro- gram for a Great Society there is an element of self-interest (though the stupid among those who will bear its cost refuse to see anything in it except an immediate outrage against themselves): self-interest, nevertheless, though of a wise and long-range kind, for no family and its children in any community can be safe from some sort of ultimate violence if conditions are ignored which let moral infection spread. But if in that sort of self-interest there is wisdom, there is also a largeness of spirit which can link our little enterprises with an idealism that comes from God. To look beyond ourselves to the needs of others, to want to help as many as we can of those who have been hurt and hindered, is to learn the spirit of Him who said that He had come to serve.

And suppose that the ideal of the Great Society should reach out explicitly beyond a nation's boundaries and its limited concerns. Already it can actually begin to do so. The economic aid extended to new and undeveloped nations and the shining example of the Peace Corps reflect a dawning awareness of the truth that "God hath made of one blood all nations of men to dwell on the face of the whole earth." When that truth becomes more fully recognized, and leaders of government and the public opinion which supports them reach out to treat all human beings as parts of a Great Society, then we shall be building something more permanent than the Babylons which perish. We may create a world community of cooperation and human helpfulness where "the glory of God is its light," and where "they shall bring the glory and honor of the nations into it."

8.

When the Brave Voice Speaks

They said to him then, "Who are you? . . .
What do you say about yourself?"

JOHN 1:22

MEN WHO thought themselves to be very important were demanding
an answer from a man whom they thought to be of no importance
at all. In the Jordan River valley a person who had never been heard
of before had appeared and begun to preach; and what he said was
startling. He declared that a day of judgment was at hand, and that
men had better make ready to face it. "The ax is laid to the root
of the trees; every tree therefore that does not bear good fruit is
cut down and thrown into the fire."

Representatives of the priests in Jerusalem had come down to
hear for themselves what this man was saying. His name was John,
and the crowds who had begun to flock around him called him
John the Baptist, because he was not only preaching but baptizing
also. But what business did he have to be doing either one? That
was what the authorities wanted to know. "Who are you?" they
challenged him. "What do you say about yourself?"

That could be a searching question; and the reply to it might
say a great deal—or perhaps next to nothing. Imagine it addressed
to us. What would each one of us answer, over and above the
impersonal listing which a census taker might write down? That
public listing might be satisfied with a single word: college student,
businessman, physician, teacher, housewife. But in intimate reality,
"What do you say about yourself?" College student, yes; but studying what, and why? Only the regimented courses which you have
to take in order to collect enough credits to graduate; or exciting
areas of knowledge into which you are led by eagerness to understand? Businessman, yes: but in addition to attending to the

necessary routine of whatever your business is and making money in it, have you any generous conception of human benefit which can come from what you do? Physician—of what sort? One of those for whom the men and women who come through the office door are only clinical cases to be dealt with indifferently; or instead one of the beloved doctors who not only by their technical skill but also by their spirit help troubled human beings to find healing? A teacher: meaning one who has let her work become no better than a hated drudgery; or one who by her imagination and devotion has made some little country schoolroom into the place where boys and girls find quickening not only for their minds but also for their souls? And the one who might be written down only as a "housewife": if she could tell the truth about herself it might be the story of the unreckoning love of which a woman can be capable, by which what might have been a barren house is made into a home that is a haven of happiness and peace.

"What do you say about yourself? Who are you?"—the *real* you whom the person outside may have no way of knowing. It is the answer to *that* question which is the decisive matter.

Listen to John's answer. "I am a voice." Do you mark the proud significance of that? Perhaps at first you do not mark it. A voice, you say; what is that to boast of? The world is full of voices. No, but it is not. Not in any such sense as was true of John. The world is full of little babblings, a confused chatter of this and that, ejaculations shrill and insistent, falsettos and discords and confusion. Only here and there out of the blur and medley rises the great note of the authentic voice. When Caruso sang, the blind could know when he appeared. Over the chorus of lesser men and women, the great voice floated, vibrant, triumphant, unmistakable. So it is also on the wide stage of practical choices and decisions, and especially in the moral and religious sphere. Over the crowd clamor or over the ineffective utterance of the unsure souls, fumbling for expression, rings the message of some great spirit who knows what he would say. For him the meaning of life is clear. Its details are swept like notes into the mightier harmony. When he speaks, men stand in hushed astonishment. When he speaks, it is as though the trumpet blew.

When John's voice began to be heard, the reverberations of it spread through all the land. "Then went out to him Jerusalem and all Judaea and all the region about the Jordan." People of all classes and conditions flocked to hear what he had to say. "A voice—crying in the wilderness": that is what he said he was. Consider the superb authority of that. He did not go to city and town, but town and city came to him. He did not run after the multitude and fawn upon them with persuasion. He stood still in the majestic confidence of his moral certitude, and the multitude beat a path through the wilderness to where he was.

John was a great figure. That is obvious; and it is inevitable that we should think of him as such. But there is danger that we may think of his greatness in terms so awesome and unfamiliar that we lose his relevance for ourselves. He was a prophet, we say; and we are apt to consider a prophet as someone with supernatural gifts, caught up perhaps in visions, endowed with divine fore-knowledge, a figure belonging back there in Bible times but not likely to be repeated in any surroundings that we know. Yet the real fact is that John the Baptist and all the others before him who were called the prophets were intensely human. There was nothing abnormal, and in most cases not even anything mystical about them. Their greatness was of the kind that can appear again in any time whenever a human soul is possessed by some immense convic-tion. In our own generation Winston Churchill had a power which had some likeness to the power of the prophets. He was so filled with a sense of the imperishable heritage of a great people, and of the demands which that heritage made upon valor and devotion, that when he spoke men heard not only an individual but the soul of England speaking. So it is with any man who brings an authentic word of truth and duty. He can be an instrument of God—and be such not the less genuinely though in his case it may be with no world-wide fame. Let a man have found some moral and spiritual certainty which has become for him imperative, let him believe with all his mind and heart that it needs to be conveyed, and that man in his place can have in his own measure the kind of impact which the prophets have always had. In his presence people may begin to feel that something irresistible is speaking to their con-science—something that carries the mighty overtone of *Thus saith the Lord*.

Remembering John the Baptist therefore not as a distant and unrelated part of bygone history but as a type of prophethood that needs continually to reappear, let us think more specifically of the facts which made him into the man that he became.

I

John "was in the wilderness till the day of his manifestation to Israel." That is to say, he had spent much of his life in solitude. So had some of his great forerunners. Elijah appeared out of the desert. So did Amos. They were not dependent upon anyone else for subsistence, or for society. Only the sun and the moon and the vast procession of the stars were their companions. No clamor of tongues could invade the silence in which their spirits chose to dwell.

Now it is true that solitude as a means for seeking God can be overdone. It certainly was in earlier Christian centuries. It began to be supposed that the supreme holiness could be attained only by fanatical extremes of separation such as those of St. Anthony and St. Simeon Stylites. The long history of monasticism reflected in part at least that same assumption. It could lead to a distortion of life—a distortion of what men ought to have learned from Jesus. He found his Father in his ministry to his human brethren. His spirit expanded most when he was in the midst of his service to the needs of men.

But if solitude can be overdone, there is not much danger of that in our modern world. The pace of existence is so hectic that there may be no time to think. In earlier and quieter times fathers and mothers and boys and girls knelt at family prayers before they started out to the occupations of the day. In how many homes can we see that now? And for how many of us is there any period at all when we clear a space of quietness in which our thought can be alone with God? The voices that might come from another world are drowned by the noises of the street. So our sense of the meaning of life may have no great consciousness round which to rally. We may become the disorganized echoes of crowd opinions because our souls are not centrally possessed. Deeply we need what John the Baptist deliberately made part of his existence: the chance for contemplation long enough and steady enough to let the heavenly purposes lay hold upon our souls.

One of the great psalms is Psalm 46, which begins, "God is our refuge and strength," and moves on toward its conclusion, "Be still, and know that I am God." It is often remembered particularly as "Martin Luther's psalm," for it was from its inspiration, and from the direct suggestion of some of its words, that Luther wrote his immortal hymn:

> A mighty fortress is our God
> A bulwark never failing.

It is true—as we recognized before—that God's fullest manifestation must be out in the stir and stress of life, where his power can fortify what men are trying to do in obedience to his will. It is there, where the fight is fiercest, that he will be the "bulwark never failing." Martin Luther knew that abundantly, as have all great virile souls. But it may be in the stillness that the awareness of God must begin—or must be recovered when it is in danger of being lost. Elijah, discouraged and dismayed, sought the quiet of the cave in Horeb; and there in his aloneness God spoke to him again, not out of the earthquake or the lightning or the rushing wind, but in the still, small voice. So also in our own century another spokesman for God knew the power that can come from quietness and prayer. Charles Henry Brent, missionary bishop of the Philippines, wrote in his 1905 Notebook, at a time when difficulties pressed upon him heavily, "We must enter heaven and sojourn in it every day in order to understand the meaning of life and do the work that lies before us. The courts of heaven are but a step away. The doors are shut neither day nor night. Anyone who believes in God can find his way to the very throne."

II

It was out of his contemplation and his contact there with God that John the Baptist got what the people most admired in him—his intrepid courage. Many different elements in the population came to hear him, and among them some whom an ordinary man would have feared to face. The Romans were the occupying power, and Roman legionaries were there in the listening crowd—legionaries who were not accustomed to straight talk from a man who belonged to the conquered people. The so-called publicans were there, tax-gatherers who had it in their power to be brutal. And most important were the Pharisees and the representatives of the Temple priests. These were the men of rank and privilege, accustomed to deference from everybody. But John confronted Roman and Jew with no distinction and with no softening anywhere of moral truth. The obvious sins deserved rebuke, and he rebuked them. But what he assailed with fiercest condemnation was the kind of sin that tried to hide behind a pious front—the sin of Pharisees and priests, of whom Jesus later was to say that they were like whited sepulchres, full of dead men's bones; for they were so avaricious and merciless that they would "devour widows' houses and for a pretence make long prayers." There in the Jordan valley these men had come to look at John and listen to him with cool arrogance, but when he saw them his wrath blazed. He would tell them what they were, and what they would look like when the time of judgment came. They would be

like a swarm of snakes trying to wriggle off to safety when a great fire
swept along the ground. "You brood of vipers!" he said. "Who
warned you to flee from the wrath to come?"

Then there was a power still more formidable than that of the
Pharisees and priests which John dared to challenge. Herod Antipas,
tetrarch of Galilee, had taken his own brother's wife and married
her. Everybody knew of it and talked about it—but not out loud.
To enlarge upon the sins of ordinary people was one thing, but to
be heard passing judgment on the sin of Herod was something else.
It could have seemed that the sensible thing also for John the
Baptist was to keep still. That is the kind of temptation which can
always come to the man who has a moral message which his conscience bids him to deliver: "Deliver it—but not to extremes where
it may do no good." Halford Luccock, with that brilliant incisiveness
of his which could drive the truth home to everyone's awareness,
expressed the fact of this temptation to evade, or at least to compro-
mise: "We are beset before and after by proverbs which whisper,
'watch your step.' We are told that 'discretion is the better part of
valor,' and what sweet music it often is to our ears! We readily forget that the epitaph on the gravestone of many good causes has been,
'Died of discretion.' We are told with unctuous persuasiveness that
'he who fights and runs away, lives to fight another day.' That is
usually a lie. He may live, only to run away again at the next
crisis."[1]

Not so with John the Baptist. No hostility from Herod or anyone
else could touch his courage, or blunt the truth he dared to speak
out. The result might bring its heavy cost to him, but he made
a whole people understand the sovereignty of moral conscience, and it
was for this that he supremely cared.

III

Consider next the thought John had of the relationship between
what God desired and what men could do. He never supposed that
human beings alone could redeem their world. Only the infinite
grace of God could accomplish that. But there was something that
men *could* do. They could look honestly at themselves and see what
their own sins were—the actual sins that stood in the way of the
purpose of God; and then they could repent, which meant to try

---

[1] *The Interpreter's Bible,* Vol. VII (Nashville: Abingdon Press, 1951), p. 735.

to turn around and go God's way instead of their own way. Nor was that all. When they saw the road of the better order of life on which God wanted them to go forward they could help to build it, to see that "every valley shall be filled," and "every mountain and hill be brought low," and "the crooked be made straight," and "the rough ways be made smooth, and all flesh shall see the salvation of God."

In our disordered and endangered present world, there does not seem to be much promise of salvation. The kingdom of God's purpose seems a long way off. All the more need therefore that from our human situation we should try to open the ways which lead in its direction. John pointed to what that direction is. "He who is mightier than I is coming," he said. The road toward the Kingdom of God would be revealed by Christ, and when Jesus of Nazareth came down to the Jordan valley and John looked into his eyes, John had the intuition that in him the Christ had come. From that time on a new faith and hope was born into the world. Through the spirit of Jesus, through his revelation of life finding its meaning in a ministry of service and through his love that reached out to all human souls, and only through that spirit, can men hope to go forward past the old sins and wrongs which have shadowed the earth.

In every time there is need of men who will have the inspired imagination that comes from Christian faith—faith that goes beyond the possibilities which the materialist and the man of the world believe in. "Where there is no vision the people perish"; but where there *is* vision, there can be accomplishments which the crowd would have held to be incredible. There have been shining examples of that on the physical plane. The men who first imagined such a thing as a transcontinental railroad to the west—spanning rivers, tunneling mountains, crossing the interminable prairies where hostile Indians could make each mile perilous—were looked upon at first as empty visionaries. So were those who dreamed that steamships could create dependable pathways across the seas. But both of these achievements have been wrought, because there were some men who trusted what at first they could not prove, and followed the foregleam of it until they turned it into fact. It is this same boldness of belief which must inspire the spiritual ventures which our human life cries out for. What we are called most to contend against are not so much material resistances, but what St. Paul called principalities, powers, and "the world rulers of this present darkness": unnecessary poverty and the degradation that comes from it, exploitation of the poor and helpless, racial injustice, blind nationalism that leads to hatred and war. Here in *this* realm is a call for men who will be sensitive to the supreme questions, and with all their hearts and minds will try to find the answers to them. What ought Christianity to mean in actual relationship to the world we live in? How can the disadvantaged be lifted out of the dark valleys in which they have been sunk? How can the mountains of entrenched selfishness which have stood across the roads of betterment be cut through? How can ancient prejudices which have twisted the approaches to truth be set straight? Here lies the challenge to every Christian thinker, and to every idealist of any name. Here in our own land sometimes, as Adlai Stevenson wrote, we may "grope in the dark." But there can come "some fresh illumination of our aims and intentions" by which "the common interests of humanity will be seized on and developed . . . so that the sense will spread through the world that the Western people are profoundly and permanently committed to the survival and dignity of man."[2]

Thus the roads of moral and spiritual advance must first come into being within the imagination of the seers, and then be projected into deliberate planned effort in which many can cooperate. It takes the great idealists to light the fire of some new possibility, but the fire will go out unless there is brought to it the fuel of a whole people's commitment to what they have been shown. A few inspired interpreters in Church and in State can help us to understand and really to desire what we pray for when we say, "Thy Kingdom come on earth"—but that is the most that they can do. *Then* comes the opportunity for all of us. The building of any road requires labor that is undramatic and may be wearisome but has nobility all the same. There is no single faithful life that does not have its part in drawing our whole existence closer to what can be its ultimate fulfillment in the purpose of God. To put the spirit of Christian consecration into some seemingly unregarded task, to sweep a room as by God's laws, to teach a school so that every spark of high desire in any boy or girl is encouraged, to carry on a man's work as stone mason, carpenter, mechanic, with such conscience for what is done that everybody seeing it can have a finer sense of what integrity can be, to make—in short—the ground of one's everyday existence firm and true, this is to "prepare the way of the

---

[2] From address before the Conference on World Tensions at the University of Chicago, May 12, 1960.

Lord," and to build a highway along which the spirit of Christ may come.

IV

All this then is what a voice like that of John the Baptist might be saying as to the possibilities of life.

And now at the end let us make sure to remember that the voice of a human soul is more than spoken utterance. "What you are speaks so loud," said Ralph Waldo Emerson, "that I cannot hear what you say"; and putting the fact more positively, what you are can speak so continually that there is no need of any conspicuous place from which to speak. A man does not have to be in a pulpit to be greatly heard. In any unplanned conversation, on the commuter's train, at the businessmen's lunch table, in a discussion somewhere about the day's news and the issues in it, the quiet words of the man who has convictions can dispense with any sounding board. If he, like John the Baptist, is concerned for the Kingdom of God, then in that steady fact he *is* a voice, and the part of the world around him, be it large or small, is better for what it hears through him.

9.

Argument, or Experience?

Our fathers worshiped on this mountain, and
you say that in Jerusalem is the place where
men ought to worship. . . . I know that
Messiah . . . when he comes, will show us all
things.

JOHN 4:20, 25

A VERY human tendency which may crop up in any one of us is to
try to dodge responsibility by starting an argument instead. To confront reality can be disturbing, especially when that reality has to
do with the relationship of one's soul to God. That is what is
illustrated in the encounter described in the fourth chapter of the
Gospel of John. Someone with whom all of us may be the more
surely identified because she is spoken of simply as *a* woman of
Samaria comes into contact with Jesus. With the insight which made
any soul be open to his deep understanding, he saw that she had a
troubled conscience. He wanted her to know that the love of God
could bring a new meaning to her life. But all that she had known
about religion made her scornful of that idea. For her, religion had
never got beyond a matter of definitions and disputes. Also, it might
be more comfortable to keep it that way instead of letting it get too
close and personal.

Such is the essential impression that comes through the Gospel
account. Let us look at its whole picture in more detail.

That Jesus should have met this woman and have had anything
to say to her might have amounted to no more than an empty
accident. But he never let an accident be empty. Wherever he was
and however he happened to be there, he seized the chance to make
that moment meaningful to somebody. This day as he was journeying
north from Jerusalem and passing through the province of Samaria,
he had come to the ancient well which tradition said had been there
since the time of Jacob; and as he rested there, this woman came out
of her village to draw water. He asked her for a drink of the water

she was drawing from the well. That request, made in such simple friendliness, was his way of opening a conversation that might lead deep into this woman's soul. She was concerned now only with the day's routine: this heavy business of coming every day to get water to carry home to cook and wash with, and back again tomorrow; this dreary round of everlasting work. That could seem all there was to life. But he would show her that there was something more. He asked her to give him a drink of water from Jacob's well; he would wake her imagination presently to understand her need of a deeper and more enduring well.

But her first response was abrupt. She looked at this traveler from Judaea and knew that he was a Jew. Why then was he speaking to her, a Samaritan? Didn't he know that with a long history of old hatreds back of them, Jews and Samaritans had no dealings with one another? Why then should he ask her for a drink of this water which belonged to her and her neighbors as a heritage from "our father Jacob, who gave us this well."

Jesus answered, "Everyone who drinks of this water will thirst again, but whoever drinks of the water that I shall give him will never thirst; the water that I shall give him will become in him a spring of water welling up to eternal life."

The woman took that quite literally. The water *she* wanted was like that in Jacob's well; only, by some happy new arrangement, flowing all the time right where she could get it, so that she wouldn't have to be coming every day to fill the heavy buckets and carry them home.

But then Jesus said something that startled her with the realization that somehow he knew more about her and about her husband— who was not her husband—than any ordinary stranger could have known. He made her conscience uneasy. He must be some kind of religious teacher, and she wasn't sure that she wanted to hear any more from him. As long as he seemed to promise some convenient new well, as real as Jacob's well and better, that would be all to the good; but this talk about the water of eternal life, that was something else again, and sounded a bit queer. How did she know, after all, that he had any authority? "Our fathers worshiped on this mountain," she said, "and *you* say that in Jerusalem is the place where men ought to worship." He had made her uncomfortable already, and now her prejudices could come to her aid to make her think that she did not have to listen to what he had to say. Her fathers and their traditions ought to be better than his. *They* must be right, and she would stand by them.

I

"Our fathers worshiped on this mountain." When the woman of Samaria said that, she said it belligerently. Attachment to old ideas could be a protective device against new possibilities of truth which could lead one further than one wanted to go. Instead of being willing to face the fact of what God might have to say to her own self, she could hide behind a discussion of what God was supposed to have said to somebody else at some other time.

The instinct of superiority in our own particular religious traditions and of dislike toward those who differ is still an entirely familiar fact. Every Christian communion has its High Churchmen who say, "Our fathers worshiped on this mountain" and are convinced that no other place or manner is fit for people to worship in. Nor is the spirit always coupled with any particular missionary zeal that the benighted persons who do not worship "on our mountain" should find their way there. Ecclesiastically a good many complacent Christians are as the Grand Lamas of Tibet used to be. They are thoroughly convinced that their particular mountains of tradition represent the nearest approach to heaven; but they are distinctly willing, meanwhile, to dwell in a sort of forbidden land. They do not want the roads to be thrown open too generously to all comers. On the whole, they prefer to maintain a select aloofness, social, sentimental, or theological, and not have too many others crowding in. As a self-satisfied ecclesiastic of eighteenth-century England wrote concerning the Methodists, and took much pride in the statement: "We have maintained an offensive attitude toward them which are without."

The stiffness with which many church people brandish this argument that "our fathers worshiped on this mountain" may lead even to the suggestion that there must be a strain of religious degeneracy among the unfortunate Christians whose fathers worshiped in any other way. People who frankly do not wish to hear the preachers of any other Christian communion, people who judge by ecclesiastical labels and put great Christian communions outside their interests because something in their method seems to their idea to be irregular, people who break their own church into factions because they insist that all others must go in with them, not only to the same temple of the fathers but through precisely the same gate of creedal interpretation and dogmatic understanding—all these stand upon exactly the same level as that upon which the woman of Samaria moved when she first looked at Jesus.

Yet, on the other hand, we shall not have seen the whole truth until we recognize that there can be a very different mood into which people can fall in regard to the mountain on which their fathers worshiped, and that in this different mood also there is danger. I think that this mood was creeping into the spirit of the woman of Samaria very shortly after she began to talk. With that bristling instinct which factional tradition always breeds, she flung the statement as to her fathers' worship against Jesus first as a challenge; but there was significance in her words, "Sir, I perceive that you are a prophet." Before the steady look of Jesus, her thought was shaken by a sudden tremor, as of a coming earthquake. She was aware that there was unsureness in what she had begun to say. Her fathers had worshiped thus and so. That was the orthodox tradition for her. That was the thing which it was her business to defend. But down in her own mind lurked the secret doubt which suddenly lay uncovered. For a while that doubt and the very necessity of smothering it may make a soul all the more relentless in its orthodoxy, just as it sent Saul of Tarsus on toward Damascus to persecute the Christians at the very time when the appeal of Christian faces like the face of Stephen had begun to stir within his soul. But often this doubt will suddenly reveal itself as a half-cynical distrust of religious reality anywhere. Thus and so said our fathers. Letter-perfect as she had been taught, the woman of Samaria flung out her formal affirmation of that. "But you say," she added to Jesus, "that in Jerusalem is the place where men ought to worship." She looked at Jesus and realized that he must be sincere. She supposed that he thought very differently from the way in which she had been taught to think. Were her fathers right? Or was he right? Or perhaps was no one right at all, and was there no dependable and certain something to be right about?

Formality in religion and the belligerent partisanship which starts out insisting that the way the fathers worshiped is the only possible approach to God may end in this sort of skepticism. We are witnessing that in our own day. For many in this generation the Christian beliefs of their forefathers are a mere empty inheritance, thin and perishable as the shell of a locust left on the ground while winter comes. The old forms are intact, but life no longer moves in and through them. Old creeds and liturgies may be admitted to be beautiful, but they do not move and inspire. Loyalty to the traditions of the forefathers may be a mere polite preference built upon a fundamental doubt as to whether there is much substance of reality to make difference important between this Christian inheritance or that. I heard a person speak with much frankness one day of another person with whom that first one was very intimately acquainted: "He goes to church every Sunday," said that devoted but somewhat sardonic intimate; "he says he believes in the Church as an institution, and he thinks it ought to be maintained; he likes its services, but as to its teachings, I do not think he believes a word of them, any more than I do."

Such a comment as that manifestly is too extreme and too tinged with a certain momentary bitterness for anyone to suppose that it is characteristic. But all of us know it to be a fact that many Christians nowadays, though they do not disbelieve the essential convictions of our Christian inheritance, yet hold them very tepidly. Often we hear men say: "Well, one road is as good as another. They all lead to the same end if a man does the best he knows." Such an easy statement as that may be in its way as shallow and false as bigotry itself. The real reason back of the easygoing indifference with which people talk of one road as being as good as another is that they have lost the passionate realization that actually there is a goal to which the roads must lead. When men are not going anywhere, or when they are not aiming at anything very difficult, then they can afford to talk lightly of all roads being alike; but the men who set out to climb Mount Everest did not talk like that. For them such a saying would have been madness and its end destruction. To reach the peak, there was a final right way and only one and, if men would scale the mountain, then along that way and along no other must they walk.

Therein lies truth that is forever valid for religious experience. There are certain choices of the soul concerning which it is a matter of life-and-death importance that one should not indifferently turn from one road to the other, but find the right one. To this road they will not bring the same experiences. They may not bring the same background of knowledge or tradition. As men from England and porters from Tibet alike walked on the same final path to Everest, so men of different traditions may walk on the same road that leads to the heights of God. They make their rest camps in different places. They may feed on different food. But for the human soul there are certain ways in which men must walk, certain great convictions of God and of the soul and of the meaning of our human life which we must find and follow if we would attain. Said that great saint of the Middle Ages, Bernard of Clairvaux, "The road winds uphill all the way; yea, to the very end." And whenever for any man life is thus an ascending quest, he must find the sure pathway of the proven spiritual convictions if he would climb. Straight is the gate and narrow is the way that leadeth unto life.

How then shall we put together the two thoughts which have been expressed? Superficially they might seem to be contradictory; but they are not. They are only two sides of the completeness of the truth. Those are wrong who think that the little particular temple of their religious inheritance, their definitions and their forms, furnish the only gateway to God; but they also are wrong who casually say that all roads of reasonably decent living will equally lead to Him. The whole matter depends upon where our eyes are fixed. If life means nothing to us but ordinary existence, with its meannesses and its mediocrities, then one road may be as good as another, since they all begin and end on the common levels; but if life means for us the striving after the highest that we know, the resolute ascent of the mountain of our souls' best possibilities, then though the roads of preparation in our inheritance lead up the lower slopes from various directions, and though we bring to the scaling of the heights our different inheritances and our various manners of dress and speech, yet on those high ranges of life's endeavor the path of truth is very simple and very narrow, and he who misses it does so at his peril.

II

We turn now to the other thing which the woman of Samaria said. "I know that Messiah is coming (he who is called Christ); when he comes he will show us all things." Here from the past she turned to the future. When God in his own good time and by his miraculous revelation showed his will, then everyone would know what he ought to do. In the meantime, there was no certain way of knowing, and every life would move on, therefore, according to the chances of the day.

There are some influences in our day which make this attitude of mind even easier for us than it was for the woman of Samaria. Our thought has been saturated by the conception of evolution, and that has led to certain curious corollaries. People have been made familiar with the idea of a cosmos which has gone rolling forward in a vast development, the progress of which has been in large measure independent of any human consciousness or direction, and implicitly they have extended that idea into other realms of life to which it has no application. With comfortable assurance many have imagined that, because the universe has gone on developing without our help in many respects, it will go on developing in all respects with an equal certainty. But the real facts completely deny any such shallow assumption. What the evolutionary process did when it produced man was to fashion a creature whose character and genius lay precisely in the fact that he, through his conscious awareness and self-direction, is lifted above the mechanical process of his world, and henceforth the making of himself and the making of a world that shall be available for his habitation depend upon the exercise of that creative mind and soul which are within him. The history of our world in this century has abundantly showed that progress for our human family is not automatic. There have been years when it seemed that civilization itself trembled on the brink of annihilation, and the dark shadow of that possibility will not move away. Before the First World War we had been letting our world drift with the assumption that civilization was bound by its own inherent force to go on developing and progressing. We thought that commerce would take care of it, that the instincts of business sagacity would save it from violence, that science would enrich it and education make men too intelligent to sink again to the level of madmen and of brutes. But in the crash of two wars that shook ordered human life to its foundations, and that make us know that another war may destroy these foundations utterly, we learned that we cannot afford to float idly into the unknown tomorrow. Every man also who looks honestly into his own soul knows the same thing. The destinies of life are determined by today. God will not save us by some act of his unrelated to our own intelligent consecration.

There are those even yet who try to be blind to that. They quibble and dispute with a childish petulance against the things that ought to be done today because they assert that the perfect idea has not been reached, and that when it is arrived at will be time enough for us to act. Stubborn men among the leadership of the nations refuse to cooperate in immediate steps toward world adjustment, and declare instead that, when this cometh, and when that cometh, and when we know everything, and it is certain that there can be no imaginable mistake, then we shall grandly proceed. Yet meanwhile, as they wait for this imaginary enlightenment, clouds of peril gather on the world horizon, and this "day of the Lord" of their postponed wisdom may be, as the prophet cried of old to Israel, "a day of doom."

So likewise in the religious destinies of our world. In this high hour of our human shaping, when the Church of Jesus Christ needs the strength of every truehearted man and woman, there are those who hold aloof in easy superiority, saying that in our divided Christendom they do not see any perfect church yet, and that they will wait for one that thoroughly suits them before they join. They are opposed to sectarianism, and so they hold aloof from such great fellowships as do exist and, by way of rebuking sectarianism, make themselves into innumerable little sects, each with a membership of one. Yet not by tomorrow's imagined illumination, but by today's grappling with the task that is before us, and with the resources that are at our hand, must life and the world be redeemed. When Messiah comes, then we shall know, said the woman of Samaria. There is no human soul for whom the Messiah ever will come unless to that soul now in the immediate present there is some high sense of accepted responsibility to the revelations which are already in our midst.

III

So we come to the climax of our thinking. At the end the woman of Samaria began to understand that the revelation of God for a human life did not have to be a misty rainbow, stretched between the horizons of the past, on the one hand, and an uncertain future, on the other. It could come to her soul—as to every soul—in an influence made immediately real to her. When she looked into Jesus' eyes, she could see that the grace of God was there. Through the interest he had had in her, through his understanding of her and his compassion for her, she could begin to think more greatly of herself. In the way he had dealt with her and in what he had said to her she had felt God's love as an expectation for her own life; and her spirit, which by itself might droop and be discouraged, could drink of that holy expectation as from a well.

"The water that I shall give him will become a spring of water welling up to eternal life." What is that water? It is like rain upon the desert that quickens the buried seeds of beauty which without the rain one would not have known were there. That is the way the encouragement of Jesus came to many of those he touched—and touches now. Peter, Matthew the tax-gatherer, Mary Magdalene—

their souls might have been forever nothing but barren ground if it had not been for him. But when he looked at them with his compassionate acceptance, with the deep gaze which saw through any evasion down to the littleness of what they really were, yet with the light that recognized and wakened the wistful desire in them to grow into something larger—*then* they knew that living waters were welling up within their souls.

So it may be always. As was true for the woman of Samaria, so for you and me by the humdrum pathways where life had seemed to become so nearly meaningless, there confronts us the figure of Jesus. We look at him and see how far away our spirit is from his. For the first time we recognize ourselves as we really are. "Come, see a man who told me all that ever I did," cried the woman to her neighbors when her conversation with Jesus was finished. So far as the record shows, of course he had not told her all that ever she did; but that was the way she felt. Before that divinely understanding gaze, it was as though every thought and feeling in every corner of her soul was visible. But the light that searched her through was not the cruel light of human criticism; it was the love of God which like the sunlight not only reveals what is, but quickens into life what is meant to be. For us, as for the woman of Samaria, that love apprehends us for itself.

We do not see Jesus standing before us in visible form, as the woman of Samaria did. But his living spirit moves in our world, and when we recognize it and are touched by it we know that life has found its meaning. Is there any one of us who has not seen men and women through whom there is transmitted to us in some real degree that which Jesus gave to the woman—a sense that the immediate reality of God has come near? Some gentle and beautiful act of mercy, some quiet spiritual heroism in which a man has conquered his own pride or resentment and has gone out to do an act of magnanimous generosity to one who had been his enemy, some valiant self-forgetting in devotion to a noble cause, have thrilled you as you watched them, and you have said that *there* was a Christ-like act. Or you have watched some invalid bear the long limitation of sickness with uncomplaining patience. You have seen the love of a mother for her children, or a woman's devotion to her husband whose unworthiness had broken down every claim except the claim of love itself which refuses to let go, and with a softening at your heart you have known that the redeeming beauty of Jesus is still present in this earth. "I who speak to you am he," he said to the woman of Samaria. The awareness of God, and of God's meaning for her life, which came to her through him, could give her the foundation on which all her thinking and her living could henceforth be built. So also his spirit speaks to us; and when our conscience listens, we know what is Christlike and what is not. Then religion becomes not an argument about old traditions, and not a postponement of conviction until everything is clear. It is a readiness in mind and heart to be responsive to the spirit of Jesus, and to believe that by that spirit our life can be made new.

10.

The Unremembered Man

Philip and . . . James, the son of Alphaeus.
MATTHEW 10:3

IT MIGHT seem that the natural words would be "the forgotten man," if we are to think of someone who is no longer within the range of general interest and not reckoned as significant. But such a person may not have been actually forgotten. It is known that he existed. It would be possible to make inquiries and find out some facts about him. But he can be unremembered, in the sense that he has seemed so unimportant that most people will not have him in their minds.

That is the way it may be with some of those listed in the Gospels as disciples of Jesus. In the roll are names which everyone with any knowledge will remember: Peter and Andrew, John, and his brother James. But what about Philip, and the other James—who in Church history is sometimes referred to as "James the Less"? Who recalls much about them? Yet they are recorded, as definitely as the men who became more conspicuous, among those whom Jesus "desired" and "appointed to be with him." Also in the Book of Common Prayer there is a special day included in the ancient Church calendar for the commemoration of these two men. The reason why they were thus linked together may be because they were inconspicuous and because we need to realize that the little man also may deserve to be remembered. Part of the life of the early Church was built on men as obscure as Philip and "James the Less."

I

Let us consider first the general fact of the value which may always belong—and that means not in New Testament times only but in our times as well—to the unremembered man.

Go into any church building which has stood for a considerable time, and what is one likely to see? On the walls tablets to those who are thought to have meant most in that church's history: ministers, elders, vestrymen, leaders in their generations. If the building itself is of special beauty, there may be a memorial to the architect. But these are not the only ones who made the church in its physical structure, and created in it whatever spiritual legacy it has cherished and handed on. We can know perhaps the name of the architect, but what of the men who laid the stones and shaped the arches? Who were the carpenters and the masons who raised the scaffoldings and set the stones in the growing walls? Who was it who perhaps one day put the cross in place at the apex of a spire? And who were the men and women who never stood in the pulpit or sat on any governing board, but who in their steady loyalty and devotion brought inspiration to the church's worship and work? You may not find their names. They are the unremembered. But they were creators, all the same.

Go into a great hospital, and what will you see there? Portraits, perhaps, of physicians and surgeons whose skill and genius made them famous, and who have been rightly honored for the knowledge and the skill they brought to the sick and suffering. But they were not alone; and what could they have done without the tireless ministry of nurses, and the work of humble persons in halls and furnace-rooms and kitchens whose unseen faithfulness kept the hospital functioning night and day?

So, even though an individual be not remembered, that assuredly does not mean that he or she has wrought nothing into a work that lasts.

No matter how high a building rises into the sunlight, its foundations go deep underground, and the higher it is the deeper and wider and more invisible those foundations are. Nothing worthwhile is accomplished in this world without the aid of men and women whose names may never have any conspicuous memorial, but who have contributed nevertheless the integrity, the faithfulness, and the everyday devotion to duty without which many of those results which seem more conspicuous could never have been achieved.

It is possible for us to be deceived by the showy things. We may imagine that the most important people are only those whose names are in the headlines of the newspapers. If a man holds high place in politics, if he is an authority in financial affairs, if he writes a great book or preaches a great sermon, we say that he is a great man. Perhaps he may be; but the most enduring greatness in any community does not depend alone on him or on others like him. For what is it that makes any period of life significant? Not a few adventures of brilliant individuals here and there, but rather the steady upward movement of a whole people. It is the creation of a general conscience which makes average men and women less ready to tolerate degradation, more responsive to high purpose, more capable of courageous belief and of sustained endeavor. We in America have dared to believe in a mighty dream, and please God that dream, in spite of some who contradict it or pervert it, shall never be defeated. It is the dream of democracy. That is not an empty word, nor a smug, cant phrase. It represents the conviction that the multitude of ordinary men have in themselves instincts of decency, fine desire, and a kind of ultimate moral daring which can accomplish something better than all the kings and conquerors would ever plan.

Those who believe this most are those who know the common people best. Go ask the social workers who see the tragedies but also the heroism of the poor. Go ask the nurses whose work takes them in and out of the tenements where the human struggle is most acute. Go ask those who have come into actual contact with groups of laboring men, fighting to win better conditions for themselves and for others like them. And what will you catch from them? You will not catch that disdain for the crowd which people who are set apart by special privilege may arrogantly express. You will not catch from them the irritated cynicism about the progress of democracy which makes some of those who are concerned only with defending their own privileges begin to play with the idea of dictatorships. No, but you will catch from them instead an admiration for the qualities of the average man, notwithstanding all the faults in our human nature; for his capacity to endure many hardships and still keep decent, for his loyalty to his family and his friends, for his willingness to go on working and sacrificing in order that his children may inherit a wider life than the one that he has known. These are the unremembered men. But they are the men who matter. They may be clerks at unimportant desks in offices, taxicab drivers, guards on subway trains, workers in factories; but out of them can proceed, and often does proceed, a wholesome purpose which justifies the hope that our social evolution has not finished, and that up from the ordinary ground of our human life clean and renewing forces can rise.

The greatness of service given to a people by what might have been the unremembered man was never more superbly symbolized than by what was done in England at the end of the First World War. There was brought from the battlefields the body of an un- identified British soldier, to be buried in the nave of Westminster Abbey, the noblest shrine of the nation's history, where kings and conquerors had been brought before. Other countries since then have followed that example, with their tombs for "the unknown soldier," but the manner of recognition wrought there in the Abbey was supreme. No ornate monument was built, no wordy eulogy displayed. Simply in the floor of the ancient and august Abbey a great flat stone was laid, telling what was buried under it, and for inscription these words of St. Paul: AS UNKNOWN, AND YET WELL KNOWN; AS DYING, AND BEHOLD WE LIVE.

Worthy almost to rank with that as a tribute to those whose sig- nificance might have been forgotten is the memorial, beautiful in its simplicity, which once stood in New York City near the Seamen's Church Institute, within a stone's throw of the waters of the port; and on it was chiseled this:

IN REMEMBRANCE OF THE
OFFICERS AND MEN OF THE MERCHANT MARINE
WHO, IN THE WORLD WAR OF 1914–1918,
WITHOUT FERVOR OF BATTLE OR PRIVILEGE OF FAME
WENT DOWN TO THE SEA AND ENDURED ALL THINGS.
THEY MADE VICTORY POSSIBLE
AND WERE GREAT WITHOUT GLORY.

This truth of the value of the inconspicuous lives can come close home to our immediate selves. There are many men and women who in every rank of life may tend to grow discouraged at what they imagine to be their unimportance. They seem to find most of their existence submerged in routine tasks. They know they are not marked out for any shining recognition in what they do from day to day. There is nothing about them that is dramatic. They are simply holding down a job which they suppose that a dozen other men could do as well. They are going through with the endless round of housekeeping or the care of little children. If someone were drawing up a list of distinguished citizens he would not mention them. Suppose that this be so. Suppose that it be so of you. What then? Are you of no consequence in determining the quality which human life will have in the place where you may be? Must you be left out of the reckoning because in some flashy record you might not be remembered? No! In the very fact of your unnoticed faithfulness you may set in motion those influences upon which everything in your place and time depends. Phillips Brooks, great Christian of a century ago, expressed the timeless truth when he said:

> It is not the most active people to whom we owe the most, . . . not those who, meteor-like, are ever on the rush for some visible charge and work. It is the lives, like the stars, which simply pour down on us the calm light of their bright and faithful being, up to which we look and out of which we gather the deepest calm and courage. It seems to me that there is reassurance here for many of us who seem to have no chance for active usefulness. We can do nothing for our fellow-men. But still it is good to know that we can be something for them; to know (and this we may know surely) that no man or woman of the humblest sort can really be strong, gentle, pure, and good, without the world being better for it, without somebody being helped and comforted by the very existence of that goodness.[1]

Men do not often stop to think of the air they breathe. They do not write eulogies to oxygen. They take it for granted, just as they take for granted every day the rising of the sun. But if they ever lost the air, or if they lost the sun, then they would remember what these meant. And there is a spirit in this world, a spirit in some of you who read these words, that is like an atmosphere from which men may draw the breath of courage and conviction, or like the sunlight by the grace of which those who never stop to think of it continually find their way. In the superficial chronicles of your world, you might not be remembered. But what of that? That which you are is wrought every day so intimately into other lives that they cannot separate it from their own existence.

There is a book written by a man of another race, Lin Yutang, a book on China entitled *My Country and My People*, and because it is about another race it helps us to understand those qualities which are not occidental but common to the human spirit everywhere. The only way, he says, of looking at any nation is "by searching not for the exotic but for the common human values . . . this boy's naughtiness, or these girls' daydreams, and the ring of children's laughter, and the patter of children's feet, and the weeping of women and the sorrows of men—they are all alike, and only through the sorrows of men and the weeping of women can we truly understand a nation." That is so. We never understand a nation, and we never understand an individual either, until we understand the

[1] Quoted in Mary W. Tileston, *Daily Strength for Daily Needs* (Boston; Roberts Brothers, 1895), p. 86.

fundamental emotions which are there; and it is among the great multitude of so-called unremembered people, among those who are too busy doing their duty to be thinking of recognition, among men who are working hard for the sake of a wife and children, among women whose love is like a steady flame that illumines a thousand common humdrum acts with beauty—it is among these that the sweetest and most regenerating influences of this our world abide.

II

Thus far, then, we have thought of our theme in general. We turn now, in the second place, to consider it more particularly as exemplified by the two names with which we began.

As types of the unremembered men we take these two particular men of whom the Church's calendar reminds us, James the Less and Philip. What have they to suggest as to some special fashion in which a man may deserve recognition larger than the casual memory gives him?

So far as James is concerned, it must be admitted that we grope in the shadows. We know nothing definite about him, and we can only guess. Perhaps the reason that we know nothing may be because he was one of those men who can never be described by anything they do, but only felt in what they are. So far as the New Testament record indicates, this James—who to distinguish him from the more important James the son Zebedee was just the little James—never accomplished any outstanding act. He never spoke any word that had unique distinction. May it be then that the reason why Jesus chose him was simply because he was good? There are people, and you and I have known them, who can be described only by that one plain word. There is in them a transparency of spirit which lets a sense of God himself come through. When we talk with them we feel the better for it. A kind of brightness shines on everyday life through them like the brightness of spring as it falls upon the ground. Because of them it is easier to believe in all hopeful and encouraging things. Perhaps James the Less was a man like that, and perhaps it was because of this that Jesus chose him.

Of the other one of these two disciples who belong among the unremembered men, we know more than we do about James. Several times in the New Testament, more particularly in the Gospel of John, there is a mention of Philip. This Fourth Gospel gives us four distinct glimpses of him and of the manner of man he was.

He is spoken of first in connection with the first appearance of

Jesus after he came out of Nazareth and went down to the Jordan valley where John was baptizing. Jesus sees Philip and says to him, "Follow me." Not long after that Philip encounters a man named Nathanael, and he gives to him this precise information: "We have found him of whom Moses in the law and also the prophets wrote, Jesus of Nazareth, the son of Joseph." Nathanael was astonished. He wanted to know whether Philip really believed that any good thing could come out of Nazareth. Philip did not enter into any highflown arguments. He made an exceedingly brief and matter-of-fact reply. "Come and see," he said.

The next appearance of Philip is in connection with the account of the feeding by Jesus of a multitude of people one day in the open country. This great crowd had followed him out of the towns when he had gone away to be alone with his disciples, and there they were as the day began to wane. Jesus turned to Philip and asked him where they could get bread so as to give these people something to eat. Philip again responded in the same precise and practical way which had marked him when he spoke to Nathanael. He looked at the crowd and did a quick sum of arithmetic in his head. "Two hundred denarii," he said, "would not buy enough bread for each of them to get a little." So many people, so many loaves to be divided up into such and such a number of pieces, so much money to buy that many loaves—thus the whole matter fell into exact figuring in Philip's mind.

Apparently it never occurred to Philip that there might be any other factor in this situation than his ordinary arithmetic. If you were going to feed people, you had to figure out how much money you had to feed them with; and if you did not have the money in hand, it was obvious that the people would not get fed. He did not seem to remember that in Jesus there might be new resources of God that could be made available. He was quite unprepared for the marvelous thing which happened when Jesus, finding through Andrew that there was a little lad there already who had a few fish and some loaves of bread, somehow produced enough so that all those people were satisfied.

The third appearance of Philip is in Jerusalem. There were certain Greeks who had come up to the city for the festival and, having heard of Jesus, they were eager to see him. They came to Philip—choosing him perhaps because he had a Greek name—and told him what they wanted. But Philip was cautious. He was not sure that these strangers and outsiders should be allowed to speak with Jesus. He left them where they were and went and took counsel of Andrew. He had to have everything certified by good advice before he was going to commit himself.

Once again from the Fourth Gospel we hear the voice of Philip. It is on the last night of Jesus' life as he talks with his disciples following the communion supper in the upper room. Jesus had spoken those immortal words beginning "Let not your hearts be troubled; believe in God, believe also in me." And he had gone on to say, "If you had known me, you would have known my Father also; henceforth you know him and have seen him." Surely, Jesus must have thought, the disciples would have understood by now what words like those meant. They must have learned that in the spirit which shone through him the living reality of God was in their midst. But Philip did not understand. "Lord," said he, "show us the Father, and we shall be satisfied." Or, to put it in other words, "Lord, let us see God just once, and we'll be content." There must have been a kind of pitying sadness in Jesus' voice as he answered, "Have I been with you so long, and yet you do not know me, Philip?" Hadn't Philip understood that when he had seen Jesus, he had seen the Father?

No, Philip could not grasp that yet. It seemed too subtle for his exact ideas. He wanted to see God in some extraordinary and overwhelming fashion different from anything he had ever seen before, a vision in the sky, a throne in heaven, a splendor surrounded by the angels. "Lord, let us see something like that just once," he wanted to say, "and then we shall really know and be sure."

Obviously, then, Philip was not any very sensitive spirit. There was nothing of the mystic about him. Although he had been with Jesus a long time, he had had no overwhelming consciousness of being admitted into a new world all full of God. He had gone plodding along with no heavenly flame kindled in his heart. He never could have preached an eloquent sermon. Very probably he would have been embarrassed if anybody had asked him to lead in prayer. Perhaps he had thought about the revelation of God as he had thought about the bread that was needed to feed the people in the wilderness. If you did not have it, you did not have it; and that was that.

Now in the history of religion it is not strange that people like Philip should be the unremembered men. We remember those who have had great visions. We remember Moses who saw God in the burning bush, and who, when he came down from Mount Sinai, seemed to the people all radiant with an unearthly light, although he himself "wist not that his face shone." We remember Isaiah whose enraptured eyes beheld in the Temple the glory of God throned among the seraphim. We think of Paul, beholding the heavenly figure of Christ as he was halted on the road to Damascus. We think of prophets and apostles whose souls were on fire with such a consciousness of God that all the words they spoke were touched with flame. We can recall these and many others in later centuries who felt so passionately about religion that they could tell about it and write about it in ways that made it glow. But what about all the other men and women who have never possessed that kind of fervent nature? What about those like Philip, whose characteristic it is to think only very plain thoughts and speak only plain and ordinary words? Have they no place in the Kingdom of God?

Yes, assuredly they have, and the evidence of this is that Jesus included a man like Philip among his nearest friends and kept him with him, faithful to the end. Philip was not given to ecstasies. He might never be outwardly very emotional. But he would say what he thought, and he would think honestly and exactly. If anybody asked him about Jesus, as Nathanael did, he would not try to preach a flowery sermon. He would tell Nathanael precisely what he had concluded for himself, and then he would invite Nathanael to come and judge for himself. If anybody asked him how you could feed a throng of people with bread, he would not reply with glittering generalities. He would figure out in his mind accurately what he saw was needed if the thing was to be achieved. And Jesus honored that sort of man and drew him into the group of those he loved and trusted most. He knew that the kind of abilities which Philip expressed are needed in the purposes of God.

There is a place for the poets; but there is a place also for those who admit that they are prosaic. There is a place for the dreamers; but there is a place also for the practical man who will figure out the practical job and proceed to do it. There is a place for those who can be enthusiastic over great conceptions; but there is a place also for those who can come with their exact calculations as to what the large idea will cost. In every family, in every community, and in every church, there may be the individual of this type. Such is the man who will patiently figure out the ways and means of getting the thing done which somebody else has dreamed. Such is the practical man who will take on himself the drudgery of details. Such is the woman who can make the small income go a long way, the housewife and the mother who can balance a small budget and by her cheerful efficiency bring a little bit of heaven down into a happy and well-ordered home. Nobody may write their names in the starry chronicles of the saints—nobody, that is, but God. But they may be there all the same, builders of the kingdom which they do not talk very much about, but which, nevertheless, they help to create, men and women who are real disciples of Christ because their honesty and their everyday helpfulness make this world a better place.

In every Christian church there is celebrated the Holy Communion. Often there are men and women who stay away because they do not think that they have any very active religious sensibility. They suppose that the only people who belong at the Communion are those who have an instinctive love for spiritual things, and who find it, perhaps, easy to pray and easy to express their inner feelings. They know this is not true of them, and so when the Communion begins they are apt to take their hats and coats and walk quietly out with the idea that the Communion belongs to the special people and they belong only to the average multitude that will be going up the street. They suppose that if Christ were calling his own disciples to draw near to him he would not remember them. But they are wrong. Their names may be James the Less or Philip. They may be quiet unassuming people, or the practical, unemotional people and, as they tend to think, the unreligious people. But for all that, their names may be written on the Master's roll.

It is to such that the message of the real truth needs to come: to you who think, but wrongly think, that in the divine eyes you are the unremembered men and women. But you are not. You who go on doing your duty and saying little about it, you whose religion may not be much more explicit than a feeling of conscience which secretly you follow, you who may never be among the visionaries, but on whose knowledge and exactness men of vision must depend, *you* have your place among the acknowledged disciples of the Lord. *You* belong at the sacrament of his presence, because you belong to him.

11.

The Woman Who Never Knew

And he saw a poor widow.

LUKE 21:2

IT WAS nineteen hundred years ago that she lived, this woman who never knew. Even now we have no record of her name. She came out of obscurity and seemed to go back into obscurity again. But for one immortal moment she stood in the gaze of Jesus; and the quality of her spirit as revealed in that one moment has made her figure stand illumined in the midst of the long dimness of the distant years, so that to the end of time she will be remembered. She did not know; but unnumbered generations have known and will know about her. She is one of the supreme examples of a life that seemed insignificant, but which, because of its character, revealed an actual significance which burns like an undying flame.

Who was this woman who never knew? Turn to the twenty-first chapter of Luke, and you will see. She came one day into the Temple in Jerusalem when Jesus and his disciples were standing there. There was a box where people put their offerings for the maintenance of the temple and its worship. All sorts of people had come past and made their gifts, and among them were some of the rich who had given largely. But the woman was not rich. She was a widow, and very poor. What she put in was in seeming value next to nothing. It was only "two mites," and a mite was the smallest of all coins in circulation. But it was all she had. The quick glance of Jesus saw what she did. His swift intuition perceived the meaning of it. He knew that through her had poured a quality of devotion lavish and beautiful beyond compare. He turned to his disciples and said: "This poor widow has put in more than all of them; for they all contributed out of their abundance, but she out of her

poverty put in all the living that she had." Yet there is no record
that he said anything to her. She passed by unconscious that this
act of hers had been marked forever as a lovely thing.

"How do we know that she never knew?" someone may object.
"How do we know that Jesus did not speak to her or send one of the
disciples to tell her what he had seen?" Because from all that we
perceive of Jesus we understand that this was not his way. He
would not have marred the beauty of her act by making it self-
conscious. In his Sermon on the Mount he had spoken of those whose
alms were in secret and whose reward from God is secret too. He
knew the blessing which was already in her heart. She had brought
a great oblation to God, and God himself would fill her soul with
his own answer. Any word of comment coming from other lips would
have been only an intrusion.

Thus it often is with the deepest and sweetest things of life. If they
are marked and exhibited, they may lose their sacredness. If it is
known that they are to become a sort of public testimony, they
would have no more the spontaneity that makes them what they
are. The love of God is too wise and too gentle to embarrass the
human soul in its most beautiful moments by calling attention to
their beauty. But let us not on that account forget that the beauty
is there. There are lives all around us every day which, though
they walk in hidden ways, are fragrant with the finest flowering of
our human spirit. There are those who may never know that others
have seen greatness in them; but in their character they go on being
great. From such as these the worth of our whole humanity proceeds.

Let us analyze now this general thought; and in relation to this
particular woman who never knew, mark what it was that made
her so worthy to be known.

I

In the first place, she had identified her life with a great interest.

She in her own personal and everyday existence might have
seemed to have no large interest. No, nor to be of any particular
interest either. She must have been among the humblest citizens
of Jerusalem, and one of the multitude of whom nobody took much
account. Nevertheless, she remembered that she was a daughter of
Israel, and all the great association of that clothed her thought with
dignity. She belonged, as we might put it in our modern words, to
the Church—the Church whose meaning stretched far out of the
past and through the present and into the future. Its inheritance was

not a distant and impersonal thing. It was hers, hers to be proud of and to live by. The worship in the Temple too was hers, and to the measure of her ability she maintained it. Her life was lifted up into the high sacredness of the life of her people as the life of that people was lifted up to God.

Can you not see the difference that this made to her? The pity of many lives is that they are unrelated to anything exalted or exalting. But her life was not so unrelated. Of so many men and women it is true that all their thoughts are thin and shrill, with no vast overtones that reach from the past and go on into the future. But with this woman it was not so. She had a spiritual ancestry, and she knew it. In the background of her consciousness stood the immemorial record of the history of Israel, the history of patriarchs and prophets, of saints and seers, of men and women who had known God and revealed him through the many generations. They had passed on a torch to her, the torch of an instinctive sense that life had been great and could be great. This remembrance out of the past gave meaning to the present. The material aspects of her existence might be drab; but above these always there was the spiritual aspect that overarched them with its infinite sky. Out of the shabby streets of Jerusalem where she lived, she could climb to the splendid courts of the Temple, and these and all that they suggested belonged to her. She could remember there that God existed and that God reigned. She could think of holiness and truth and beauty. She could walk there with a heart that sang: "O give thanks unto the Lord, for he is good: for his mercy endureth for ever." And as she tarried in the Temple before she went down again to the humdrum ways, she could remember the high promise: "The eternal God is thy refuge, and underneath are the everlasting arms." Nor were the past and the present all. There was a future too. The faith of Israel always looked ahead toward a brightening horizon. What God had wrought in the past was glorious; but what he was still to accomplish would be more. Some day the Messiah would arise. God would send the Savior and Deliverer of his people. Always ahead there was the hope of a better time, a larger life, a sweeter and a kinder world.

Is it not clear that in our own day, exactly as in that distant time, it is possible for lives otherwise obscure to be exalted because they identify themselves with the great associations of religion? Look, for example, at that great communion which is a part of that Christendom to which we all belong, the Roman Catholic Church. We may regard it as in serious respects in error. But through its life great spiritual realities shine. Go into a Roman church in the slums of a city; or go into one of those agelong shrines that tower over the houses of some ancient town of Europe, like the Cathedral at Chartres. All day long you will see innumerable humble people coming to kneel there in the quiet and to say their prayers. The houses where they live and the shops where they work may have little beauty in them; but into the church they come to find beauty and spaciousness and that brooding sense of mystery and awe within which their spirits may expand. They may never be known in the chronicles of the world; but in the long run their lives will be better because they have breathed the air that blows from the heights of the consciousness of God.

So ought it to be with us and with all Christian people. So it can be in every church which is open, as all churches ought to be, throughout the week. Go through its doors and almost always you will find some individual, or several, kneeling or sitting silent in the pews. And there, of course, on Sundays and at other times of corporate worship are the many who gather together seeking God. Something comes into lives from contacts such as these. Men and women of today begin to know that they are part of the fellowship of the ages. They bow beneath the hovering presence of the communion of the saints. Life which devoid of religion can become for all of us so hectic and so petty is linked again with its infinite significance. We remember that it neither began nor ends with the little matters of today. It can feed upon all the rich inheritance of those who have gone before. It can enlarge by its present faithfulness all that is to come hereafter. Time becomes part of eternity. The little cares, the sharp anxieties, the lonely sorrows, the problems wrestled with in secret, become no longer lonely. They are swept into the deeper music of God's meaning for all life. We know that somehow all that we are and all that we do are part of his purpose; and knowing that, we can go on to the routine of the common day with lifted eyes and braver hearts.

Surely there is nothing that our generation more acutely needs than this sense that life can be linked with great associations and with great commitments. I remember once hearing a famous preacher speak to the students of Harvard College at a weeknight meeting in the Harvard Union. After he had held them fascinated with a long account of his own life and work, he sat down amid tumultuous applause. And then leaping to his feet again, he added one startling sentence. "Boys," he said, "there is one more thing I want to say. Join the Church and go into politics." What did he mean by that?

This is what he meant, that they ought to be identified with a great fellowship of loyalty that would link their own souls to the great souls of yesterday and today and tomorrow, and that then, in the light of this loyalty they should go out and express it in their active lives. They must be better citizens and more useful members of their communities. They must take their manly part in weaving the common fabric of our life more close to the pattern of God.

It is a call such as this that ought to go out to all young men and women today, bewildered and disheartened as many of them are by the confusion of existence and the seeming lack of any guiding lights. They must be called to fellowship with what the Church ideally is: namely, the great company of all faithful people, the people, that is to say, who keep the faith with all that is best in our human yesterdays and pass that fire on, the brighter because of their own courage, to light the days that are to come. And if all this seems to have carried us a strangely long distance from the woman in the Temple at Jerusalem concerning whom we started out to think, then we are mistaken, for the thought with which we began and the thought that we are following now belong together. That woman's life became significant first of all because she did not live in the little round of the commonplace, but had interests that took her up into the wider orbit of concerns that had in them the greatness of God. And if any life today is to be significant, it must be moved by exactly that same spirit. It must be trying to identify itself in imagination and in loyalty with something that is big enough to stimulate its biggest and its best.

II

We pass on now to a further consideration. That woman whom Jesus looked upon was worthy of the honor he gave her because she not only had an interest but also did something about it.

How easy it might have been for her to say that there was nothing worthwhile that she could do. There were the rich men who came into the Temple. They could bring large gifts out of their large possessions. If they did, then the needs of God's house would be met. It could not make any material difference whether she gave or whether she failed to give. What she could do was so small as to seem contemptible. So she might have thought and said.

Always there is the temptation to despise the undramatic thing. "What is the use of our beginning," we say, "when the beginning is so small?" "What is the use of our trying to help in anything im-

portant when our resources are so unimportant?" Some will answer
their own question with a flabby negative and lose, therefore, the
chance for the miracle of spiritual increase which can take a small
offering of money and of life and lift it into greatness. There may
be many who have heard at least the name of a woman whose
signal contribution to her time came out of the fact that she dared
to use in the beginning the little that she had. Miss Martha Berry established for the mountain boys and girls of Georgia the Berry Schools
which now are justly famous. Now they have a great circle of ad-
mirers, of friends and helpers. Now they are established on a scale
that makes them conspicuous in the public eye. But how did
they begin? They began because she had the courage and the devotion to gather together a few of the mountain children and teach
them in an outbuilding on her own land. "It is not easy," she said,
"to begin something at home. There is no glamour in just going
across the road."

How true that is! If we had something that did have glamour
about it, then we would start on that shining way, we think. If there
were something great and exciting to do, then we would rise to do
it. But the little venture, the little faithfulness, the little gift of what
we have and of what we are, why should we think that these make
any difference? Yet out of such as these the invisible treasuries of the
grace of God are filled. Out of such as these proceed those streams
of inspiration by which life and the world ultimately are exalted.

In the life of any church there are names of officially appointed
leaders that will be recorded. Some others whose names are linked
with this or that special benefaction may be recorded too. But when
all is said and done, let us not imagine that the supreme strength
of any church is summed up in these. No, its strength is in the great
fellowship of men and women, whether or not they ever know it and
whether or not their names are known, who have put the seal of
truth on their loyalty by bringing the gift of the best they have on
its behalf. These are the men and women who say in their hearts, "I
love the church," and then proceed to do something real about
it—a something not less real and not less far-reaching though it be
quiet, modest, and unassuming. They know that regularity in at-
tendance at the time of worship is not simply an individual matter,
but that it adds to the morale of all the group. So when the time of
service comes, they are there. They learn from a Sunday notice,
or in some other way to which their attention is alert, of a way they
can help in the church's work, and they come and say, "I am here
if you want me." They know that the church must have the gifts not of

the few but of the many, and so they are not ashamed to bring the little they can afford. They have made their loyalty a living thing, exactly as did the woman whom Jesus looked upon in the Temple, and though they may never know all the spiritual influences that go out from their lives, God knows and he does not forget.

III

In the third place, the woman in the story was significant because her devotion was complete.

It is a curious fact that sometimes people like to suppose that they can become like the widow by pretending to do what she did, when actually they miss completely the reality of what she did do. Materially speaking, she gave very little. They can copy that; and if her small gift won the praise of Jesus, why then is not the small gift always praiseworthy? May it not, indeed, seem all the more virtuous to contribute little and thus be unassuming? Consequently a church or some other organization for unselfish service may receive a letter from a donor which begins—with pious parroting of the word used in the long familiar King James translation—"I send my *mite*," whereas it is well known that that particular donor could give greatly if devotion once were stirred.

"I send my mite." Is it not what the widow did upon whom Jesus looked with proud and loving eyes? No, it is not what she did, for she, as is often smoothly forgotten, put in not her mite but *two* mites. Furthermore, as Jesus went on to say when he compared her with others who seemed to be great givers but were not, she had put in more than all the rest; for they gave of their abundance, but the two mites—the two copper coins which she gave—were "all the living that she had."

Here, in other words, was one who dared to be wholehearted. When she expressed her loyalty, she went the whole way.

Wholehearted dedication to something bigger than oneself is always inspiring to see. Anyone who is in intimate touch with the life of a church or of some noble philanthropy will be both exalted and humbled by the kind of gifts, out of all expected proportion, which may come in from the relatively poor. The total which they contribute may not add up to any large amount, may not seem to make a decisive difference in the organization's financial power. But the spirit which has flowed from them can lift a whole group of people to new levels of commitment to the work they will try to do together.

From many areas of life there may come—and sometimes it would seem quite accidentally—a revelation of the difference between persons which makes some of them seem small and some of them seem great; the difference between having or not having the devotion which will go all out to help and serve what they have once espoused.

One day in the *New York Times* some years ago there was a column-long article on the choice made by a West Point graduate who had been captain of the football team at the Academy. He had been solicited to get out of the army and come to be a football coach at an American college, with lavish salary. He noted the small pay he would get as a "Second Lieutenant in the regular army," and then he went on to reason thus:

This means that for many years I would live in the state of genteel poverty. In justice to myself I feel that my best interests lie in leaving the service. . . .

On entering the Military Academy I signed an agreement, as do all cadets, to remain for four years at West Point and a subsequent four years in the regular army. The War Department, however, during the past few years has accepted resignations of recent graduates when unusual circumstances exist. My financial prospects in civil life are so far superior to anything I can ever obtain in the army that I believe they constitute unusual circumstances.

So he made his decision "in justice to myself" and "my best interests." On *that* basis, it all seemed logical. To make more money —what was that but common sense? So be it; but it is doubtful if anyone who read his words had a higher opinion of human nature because of them.

But there are some men who do embody in themselves and reveal to others the higher reality of what a man can be. At the end of the war of 1861–65, General Samuel Chapman Armstrong found himself at Hampton, Virginia, in the midst of thousands of poverty-stricken uneducated and confused ex-slaves. He might have said that the first thing to do "in justice to myself" and "my best interests" was to go somewhere else. But what he did was to start to build a school for newly enfranchised Negroes and for Indians, the two groups that had least and needed most. He had nothing to build it with, but he would build it because it ought to be built and therefore in his faith could be built. "There's work here, and brave souls are needed," he wrote to a possible teacher whom he wanted to enlist. "If you care to sail into a good, hearty battle . . . if you like to lend a hand where a good cause is short-handed, come here." In the face of hostility and through many hardships, he did build the school which was to grow great as Hampton Institute. And this is what he wrote:

A work that requires no sacrifice does not count for much in fulfilling God's plans. But what is commonly called sacrifice is the best, happiest use of one's self and one's resources—the best investment of time, strength, and means. He who makes no such sacrifice is most to be pitied. He is a heathen because he knows nothing of God. It pays to follow one's best light—to put God and country first; ourselves afterward.[1]

Or consider a figure even nearer to our present time. In 1965 there died Dr. Gordon S. Seagrave, who never had and never sought the kind of rewards that many men strive for. Born in Burma of a line of missionary forebears, the first of whom had gone from America in 1834, he came to Johns Hopkins University to study medicine. When he graduated in 1922 he might have stayed in the homeland, where life would have been comfortable and secure. Instead he went back to Burma, with no possessions except some cast-off surgical instruments which he picked out of a wastebasket in the Johns Hopkins operating room; and these were the best he had when, back in Burma, he went from Rangoon to Mandalay, up the Irrawaddy River, and then with Chinese coolie carriers up the remaining length of Burma, through tiger and leopard country, to Namkham, at the northeast border next to China. There he inherited what passed as a hospital, a rotting wooden building in the jungle, with twenty bare, wooden beds.

For more than forty years he would be there, and it was there that he would die. Gradually he built new buildings, from the stones which he and his few helpers carried up out of the mountain riverbed. He trained a body of nurses whom he recruited from among the surrounding peoples who had never before known the meaning of education—Burmese, Kachins, Karens, Shans: girls, of whom he would later write in *Burma Surgeon*, who, "astonished to be treated with respect, . . . tried all the harder to deserve respect. Receiving affection, they became worthy of affection." They had come out of a primitive environment, knowing nothing of what the regimen of a hospital ought to be. But they "did try," wrote Dr. Seagrave; "bathed and bathed and bathed—until they were as clean

---

[1] Edith Armstrong Talbot, *Samuel Chapman Armstrong* (New York: Doubleday, Page & Co., 1904), pp. 299, 301.

and sweet a group of girls as you could find in any country."[2] He was their "Daddy," and under the stimulus of his expectation they responded with eagerness to learn.

There, alone and almost unheard of by the world at large, Dr. Seagrave ministered to the sick who flocked to him from the jungle villages. Then, in the course of the Second World War, there flooded into Namkham the backlash of sick and wounded from the Chinese armies trying to protect the Burma Road. After that, the approach of the Japanese; the hospital bombed and evacuated; Seagrave and his nurses joining the remnants of the Chinese forces, under the command of General Joseph W. Stilwell who had been sent from the United States to the aid of China, in retreat across the terrible mountains of North Burma through matted jungle trails, to India. Back over the same trails again as the fortunes of the war reversed, back this time to find only ruins at Namkham—and to build the hospital up all over again.

By then, Seagrave and his nurses were famous. He was recognized as one of the great physicians of the world. He might have said, as the young West Point graduate did, "My best interests lie in leaving the service." But the service *he* had taken up he would not leave. And his son, who came to him from America shortly before he died, could write of him:

He did not have to stay at the end of the world. He could have fled after one of his overwhelming disappointments. He could have returned to a brilliant career and earned a fortune—and died comfortably surrounded by family and friends in any placid suburb.

Instead he had renounced the comforts of the outside world, renounced even friends and family to live for many years alone in pain and privations.

"The only way the people of Burma will ever believe that I meant what I've done is for me to die here among them." That was his only answer when a well-meaning American pleaded with him to seek medical care, or at least a rest, "back home."[3]

So it was in Namkham that he died. And when he was buried by the hospital, an unending crowd, estimated at twenty-thousand, streamed in from the mountains and the jungle to stand about his grave.

[2] *Burma Surgeon* (New York: W. W. Norton & Company, 1943), p. 40.
[3] Sterling Seagrave, "Burma Surgeon: A Farewell," *Washington Post,* June 22, 1965.

Who can doubt where Gordon Seagrave and Samuel Chapman Armstrong and others—known or unknown—who have been like them stand in the reckoning of God? They are the great souls because they have been wholehearted.

Nor have they been without the reward that is greater than anything the world can give: the inner reward of the love and gratitude which must pour in on souls that have set no limit to their service.

12.

Martha and Mary

A woman named Martha received him into her house. And she had a sister called Mary, who sat at the Lord's feet and listened to his teaching.

LUKE 10:38-39

ONE MORNING an alertly interested member of the church congregation came into the parish house, and lost no time in expressing what was in her mind.

"I am worried about Martha," she said.

"Martha? Which Martha?" I asked.

"The Martha in the Bible," she answered. "I have been reading about her in the New Testament, and here is what it says. Jesus went into a village, and then 'A woman named Martha received him into her house. And she had a sister called Mary, who sat at the Lord's feet and listened to his teaching. But Martha was distracted with much serving, and she went to him and said, "Lord, do you not care that my sister has left me to serve alone? Tell her then to help me." But the Lord answered her, "Martha, Martha, you are anxious and troubled about many things; one thing is needful. Mary has chosen the good portion, which shall not be taken away from her." '

"Now I do not see why Jesus said that Mary had chosen 'the good portion,' as though what Martha was doing was not good. Why was it right for Mary simply to sit at Jesus' feet while Martha did all the work, and for Jesus apparently to approve it? It seems to me that Martha was the one who was doing what needed to be done, and ought to have had the praise instead of Mary."

So she said, and of course it was plain to see the question which concerned her. She was not thinking primarily of that particular Mary and Martha who lived far off yonder in Bethany nineteen hundred years ago. They were types and names for nearer people. She was thinking of those among our contemporaries and friends—

yes, of those elements within ourselves—which are like the two sisters of Bethany. Why do some people have to go on doing the world's work while other people seem to be the ones who get appreciation?

That is a fair and honest question. It is often asked, and asked not only by and about women but by and about men also. Let us consider it now, and let us begin by seeing—

I

The picture of Mary and Martha as most people see it.

Here then the picture is. Jesus comes to the village of Bethany late in the day, and he goes to this house of his friends, where he knew he would be welcome. He was weary perhaps. It may be that he was hungry too, after a crowded day of which it might have been said, as it was said once of another day, that he and his disciples "had no leisure so much as to eat." Obviously the thing to give him then was hospitality. And who gave that hospitality? Martha. It was Martha who bestirred herself in the kitchen, Martha who got together the best the house could afford to make ready with lavishness for Jesus. To light the fire and boil the water and fix the food was prosaic business. It did not look devotional, like going to church. But somebody had to do it, and Martha was the one who did. And, meanwhile, where was Mary? It looked as though if that evening meal were to be made ready most quickly and most attractively four hands were better than two. But Mary's hands were not there helping Martha. They were folded in her lap. There she was, as Martha looked to see, sitting at Jesus' feet and listening to Jesus as he talked to her—as he told her, perhaps, where he had been that day and what he would do when he went up presently to Jerusalem.

To Martha, and to many of us when we are in the mood of Martha, that looked like an unfair arrangement. All the more so when Jesus turned aside Martha's suggestion that Mary be told to get up and bestir herself and come and help her. Surely, Martha thought, the work she was doing at that moment was more important than anything else could be.

That is what people often think. Here, for example, is a man who is the father of a family. He feels convinced that what he does is the basis of that family's existence. He earns the money to maintain the house. He furnishes the economic undergirding for everything. Without him, without the long hours he puts into his profession or into the exacting routine of a business office somewhere, there would be no house for the family to live in and no food for them to eat. He may be annoyed when the rest of the family do not seem to recognize this. He grows so intently convinced of the prime importance of earning money that he may resent the fact that other members of the family seem to have divergent interests. He wants his sons to go into the same sort of business he is in. He wants them to make a financial success, as he has. He wants them to feel sympathetic with himself and to like the kind of things he likes. In the round of his intense and practical energy, he thinks his sons ought to be with him and share the associations which he has made supreme. When they do not, he is bewildered and hurt. Because they appear to have other preferences that lead them away from him, he may think that they are unappreciative of all that he has done to furnish the foundations for their own lives, inclined instead to other sorts of enthusiasms which seem to him impractical, presenting in their difference almost a rebuke to the things which he has done. If somewhere in his troubled heart he has a prayer, it will be something like this: "O God, make them come back to me; make them want to do what I think is important and what I want."

Or here, somewhat less frequently, is a similar feeling of a mother toward her daughter, or her son. Now and then we see women whose strongest impulse is to monopolize their children. Perhaps there is an only child, or the other children have married, and only one is left. Then the mother may make upon that one child demands which are imperious and ruthless, and no less so for the fact that they are under the guise of devotion. The mother may absorb that child's entire time and energy into her own circle of desires. With a completely unconscious selfishness she may contrive to make it seem that the child would be selfish if it followed at all its own independent instincts for life. That son or daughter must not marry, because that would be desertion of the mother. There must be no going off to great new relationships to satisfy one's own soul. The business of the child is to help the mother do what *she* thinks the other ought to do.

Or take the same sort of feeling in its wider aspects. There are thousands of us everywhere who in our general estimate of the duties and responsibilities of our world reflect instinctively the values of Martha. We say that the world's work gets done by the practical people. We may be scornful of those we call the dreamers and the idealists. The thing to do is to get down to rock-bottom reality, to make money, to keep the wheels of business going, to be practical all the time. Every now and then, for example, one will hear some loud note like this sounding in the field of education. Politicians appealing to the ordinary man's vote will denounce the curriculum in certain schools and colleges. "What is all this nonsense about classes in music and art? All such frills and flummeries should be denounced. The only thing that matters is sound vocational training, to teach boys and girls how to get a job most quickly and fit smoothly into the industrial machine." And even in the field of religion the same idea may appear. In the minds of many persons, who is the most successful ecclesiastical leader, the most satisfactory parish priest, the most effective bishop? It is the one who can bring in the largest contributions, balance the budget most surely, build the most conspicuous new buildings. "Well, are you not obliged to have these things if you are going to do your work properly?" they demand. "Are not these just as much a part of necessary existence as eating three meals a day? Dreaming and imagining and listening to large ideas may be all very well; but when things come to the pinch it is Martha who matters. If we are going to have anything for ourselves and anything to give to others, we have got to get up off our knees and go to work."

Indeed, this glorification of the spirit of Martha can become almost a religion in itself. Kipling expressed that religion with a kind of scornful denial of what he thought is its too easygoing opposite, in his ballad "The Sons of Martha."

> It is their care in all the ages to take the buffet and cushion the shock.
> It is their care that the gear engages; it is their care that the switches lock.
> It is their care that the wheels run truly; it is their care to embark and entrain,
> Tally, transport, and deliver duly the Sons of Mary by land and main.
>
> .   .   .   .   .   .
>
> And the Sons of Mary smile and are blessed—they know the angels are on their side.
> They know in them is the Grace confessed, and for them are the Mercies multiplied.
> They sit at the Feet—they hear the Word—they see how truly the Promise runs.
> They have cast their burden upon the Lord, and—the Lord He lays it on Martha's Sons!

II

We pass on now to the second stage of our thought and look at the picture as Jesus saw it.

We note at the outset the error which almost all of us fall into when we recount the story of Mary and Martha. My visitor said she did not understand why Jesus said that what Mary did was better than what Martha did. As a matter of fact, he did not say so. What he did say is quite plain, and it is different. He said Mary had chosen the "good portion." He did not make any implied comparison or condemnation of the part of Martha. He simply said that Mary had made her own choice, that it was a good choice, and that she must not be denied it.

But how was it even a good choice? one might ask. Was she not obviously neglecting her duty to be helping Martha? How could it be a good thing to be the sort of person who sits down listening enjoyably while someone else does the work?

The trouble with this question is that it also is based on a false premise. It assumes that Mary customarily and continually did nothing while Martha did it all. Obviously, however, that was not true. Martha appeared to be irritated and surprised that Mary this particular night was not helping. She expected her to help, and the reasonable assumption is that ordinarily she did, and that is why Martha was upset when now she sat apart. We can believe this the more confidently because of what we know of Jesus himself. He was no impractical spectator of life, touching it idly on its surface like a butterfly. He dealt all the time with its solid realities. He chose his nearest friends from those who did the world's rough work. It is not likely that he would have commended Mary had Mary been the sort of person unimaginative readers of the story might think she was; namely, a large-eyed, vague, and emotional somebody who never took her share in the day's duties, but idly indulged herself in ineffective sentiment.

No, the meaning of the story lies in understanding the vivid and immediate values which it involved. We cannot understand it if we read it as a generality. We can only understand it as we enter with all our thought and appreciation into the living facts of that particular place and time. Here was Jesus at no ordinary moment of his life. He had come now to the borders of Jerusalem. There on the hill beyond Bethany the great city waited, tremendous, tragic. He knew that presently he was going up there to confront his enemies in the very citadel of their power, to put his ministry to the final test, to run the risk of rejection, defeat, and death. Already there stole toward him the imagined shadow of the cross. And now tonight he had come into the house of two of his friends whom he believed to be nearest to him in loyalty and understanding. Perhaps he was weary of body, and so he would be grateful for rest. Perhaps he was hungry and so he would be grateful for all Martha's busy and generous haste to get him supper. But these were not all the needs he had, and they were not the deepest. It was not his body's hunger that mattered most, but rather the hunger of his heart. He had his own lonely courage which if need be was sufficient; but he wanted also the warmth of comradeship as he looked at the difficult way ahead. He had his own clear purpose that nothing could dismay; but he knew that in the love of friends who understood there would be the power of an added certainty. All this he was seeking as he crossed the threshold of the home in Bethany. Martha might have understood him if she had stopped to think. But she did not stop to think. As the Gospel says, she was not only quick to serve but she was "cumbered with much serving." She was too flustered with her own plans to be sensitive to what Jesus at that moment felt. Food and drink—that was as far as her imagination traveled. But Mary was more clairvoyant. She perceived that when Jesus came there that day he wanted something more than the hospitality of the kitchen. He wanted the awareness of their hearts. That was why listening to him was a far greater welcome at that moment than filling dishes. Hers was a good part indeed, and it should not be taken away from her.

When Jesus went up to Jerusalem, and when not many days after he went out to his crucifixion, what would he have remembered to his soul's comfort then? Would he have remembered the taste of Martha's food? Hardly. He would have remembered and been grateful for Martha's eagerness to welcome him in the best way which she at that moment knew. But he would have remembered better the look on Mary's face which made him know that his mission to reveal God to human souls had not been in vain, and that here was one who understood the deeper purposes for which he lived and died.

III

We have thought of the picture as we ordinarily see it, and we have thought of the picture as Jesus saw it. Let us think now finally of the synthesis between the two.

If we read the story rightly, we shall not lose any of the values which from different aspects have been seen. To begin with, we shall not lose the honor which is due to Martha and to Martha's sons. Jesus, as we have already recognized, did not forget it. He did not disparage her, nor ever, even by implication as some have supposed, say that her contribution was unworthy. He merely said that it was not all.

No, the place of the sons of Martha in our world is certainly not unworthy. On the contrary, it is necessary, and it is noble. By and large, and from day to day, the world does rest on the sort of activity which Martha represented. There does need to be the faithful routine devotion which understands that people have got to be sheltered and warmed and fed. It would be a poor, thin sort of religion that drew a hard line between the sacred and the secular and imagined that religion consists altogether in going to church and saying prayers and looking ascetic while the activities that men and women follow as they guide the plow or run the railroad train, or keep a shop, or cook a dinner, are nonreligious. It can be true, as Browning sang, that

> All service ranks the same with God,
> With God, whose puppets, best and worst,
> Are we: there is no last nor first.

Let us remember then that the man who goes unostentatiously about his business of making a living for his family, keeps to a job when he would want to drop it, carries on when he might want to stop, and does it all simply because he has to in order to earn an income for his wife and family—this man has at least the beginning of religious loyalty, for he has already a loyalty to something larger than himself. So also the men who plan the world's great enterprises and make it possible for the ground to grow more and the factories to produce more, and multiply thus the goods which the millions will consume— these men too have their place in the plans of God. They may not always be conscious of the essential dignity that may belong to what they do, and if so it is their own personal loss. But all work well done for honorable motives and useful ends is a part of the service of the sons of Martha which Christ himself would be swift to recognize. Be glad in your own hearts then for whatever you are doing which feeds in even the simplest way the divine possibilities in our world.

But remember that this is not all. As we have tried to enter imaginatively into the spirit of Jesus that evening in Bethany, we know that the meal which Martha made ready, no matter how perfect a meal it might have been, could not have been all he wanted then. How true that is in human relationships everywhere and always, and how sad the consequences are when we do not understand it! A woman, for example, may have in her house a guest whom with all her heart she wants to make happy there. But her idea of giving that guest a welcome is to get every corner of the house so attractive and to make the dinner so lavish in menu and so elegant in service that the guest will be overcome with the perfection of it all. But though the guest may go away with admiration for her hostess' skill, it will be perhaps with no more than that; for all the while she may have been intuitively compelled to see that what her hostess and friend was really most interested in was not in *her* but rather in her praise of the elaborate hospitality. And, on the other hand, there are homes into which one goes where no hectic preparations have been made but in which one feels the serene spirit of an understanding welcome by which one's own heart is warmed.

A man thinks he has given everything that was rightly to be expected to his sons. Has he not made a home for them? Has he not sent them to school and college? Has he not paid their bills? Why should they not be grateful, and not only be grateful; why should they not be drawn to him in instinctive and affectionate comradeship? The reason is that like Martha, cumbered with her much serving, he never stopped to understand the deeper fact. When those boys were growing up they needed something more from him than the money which provided their necessities. Shyly, perhaps, they came to him with their questions, with their instinctive and unconfessed hero worship, and were rebuffed by his preoccupation. They needed the warmth of a father's friendship, and all they got was funds. And so the pathetic result may be that he, like Martha, is left alone.

So also in the conduct of those enterprises which are wider than the family home the same fact holds true. It is a great thing for any man to be one of the practical builders of the world's welfare. It may seem to a man that he has done an altogether fine and sufficient work, for instance, when he has built up a great industry, employed many men, perfected devices for what he thinks will be their physical and intellectual benefit, and created all sorts of model innovations in his industrial town. He may think his workmen ought to be entirely grateful, and he is bewildered and angered if they are not. What may be the trouble? The trouble is, perhaps, that he has been so preoccupied in carrying out the plans for what he thought they ought to want that he has not stopped to find out what they really did want. He has kept them at arm's length and handed out benefits. He has not known them as a man knows men nor sought to see things through their eyes and to feel things through their emotions. So in the end, perhaps, he fails to give them anything that is ultimately significant either for his satisfaction or for theirs.

But, on the other hand, in the relationship of a man to his sons, or a man to his associates or his subordinates, how beautiful it is when the reverse is true; namely, when a man who has not much of a material kind to give does give himself so completely that those whom he touches are drawn to him in a bond of affectionate confidence that nothing can break.

And if this can be true of men, more familiarly and more widely it is true of women. Always and everywhere there are women beyond counting whose days are so taken up with common tasks—the chores of a farm kitchen, the routine of a schoolroom, the endless details of existence in the city, buying food and cooking it, cleaning a house, washing little children's clothes—that it might seem that there is no more that they could do and nothing else that they can give. But how different often is the fact! To the part of Martha they manage to add also the part of Mary, until the prosaic tasks are made beautiful by the love and imagination which remembers always what are the real values of life. The young Alice Freeman, afterwards to be Alice Freeman Palmer, and president of Wellesley College, found herself in what were often the overburdened duties of teaching in a girl's school; but though there were times when she was "weary and sad," she had a purpose which could bring light to even the grayest days. She wrote to a friend:

As I lived among those young people day after day, I felt a want of something . . . a something I must call heart culture, in lack of a better name. . . . Looking on and into them. I said, I will try to be a friend to them *all,* and put all that is truest and sweetest, sunniest and strongest that I can gather into their lives. While I teach them solid knowledge and give them real school drill as faithfully as I may, I will give, too, all that the years have brought to my own soul. God help me to give what He gave—myself—and make that self worth something to somebody; teach me to love all as He has loved, for the sake of the infinite 'possibilities locked up in every human soul.[1]

To give not only the work of their hands, but "all that the years have brought to my own soul"—that is what wives and mothers who have made their homes a place of benediction have been enabled by the spirit of Christ to do. In that exquisite little book, *Margaret Ogilvy, By Her Son,* J. M. Barrie has written of what his mother meant to him. He tells of all the tireless things she did, but above all

---

[1] George Herbert Palmer, *The Life of Alice Freeman Palmer* (Boston and New York: Houghton Mifflin Co., 1908), p. 75.

he tells of what she was. In her eyes, he said, "I have read all I know and would ever care to write. For when you looked into my mother's eyes you knew, as if He had told you, why God sent her into the world—it was to open the minds of all who looked to beautiful thoughts. . . . Those eyes . . . have guided me through life, and I pray God they may remain my only earthly judge to the last."[2]

Such, then, I think are the answers that come to us from the thought that we have followed. The truth here, like all great truths, is not onesided but round. It does not separate the spirit of Martha from that of Mary. Both are needed if life is to be made full and beautiful; and perhaps the only reason why the second is needed more is because it is more easily forgotten. Once into that home in Bethany the Reality of God as embodied in Jesus entered, and found the welcome which one of the two who met him there could not alone express. And if in our homes and if in our places of business today the divine meaning is really again to enter in and be recognized and welcomed, we must have not the spirit of Martha only or the spirit of Mary only, but both. We must be ready to serve the spirit of God in a faithful devotion in routine things; but, beyond that, we must be quick to see through the routine the changing needs of human souls, and be sensitive to these.

2 (New York: Charles Scribner's Sons, 1901), p. 5.

13.

Before It Is Too Late

The door was shut.
MATTHEW 25:10

THOSE FOUR short words reflect the jolting reality which everyone sometimes experiences. A part of life comes to its end. A vista which had been open is open no more. The door is shut.

It is from one of Jesus' parables that the words come. The parables are pictures of life so typical that we can see ourselves in them as surely as though they spoke our names. The framework of the picture may belong to another time, the scenery may be different, but the human facts which confront us are not changed by change of time. In this particular parable which the Gospel of Matthew records Jesus describes a wedding feast as it might have been in Palestine long ago. Bridesmaids are waiting for the bridegroom to appear. They have lamps to carry in the wedding procession. But some of them have let their lamps go out, and when the word comes that the bridegroom is approaching and they go distractedly here and there to get more oil, they cannot get it; and when they come at length to the door of the house where the wedding was to be, it is too late.

I

Such are the details of the old world picture. But the details do not matter. The heart of the parable is in the fact that life does have its finalities. There are opportunities which if we did not make the most of them when they were open will not be open any more.

Let us therefore think first, as vividly as we can, of the loss that always comes when doors are shut. Then we shall consider the kind of experience of shut doors for which we, like the bridesmaids in the parable, would be to blame, and which if we are forewarned we might prevent.

In all life there is an element which is inexorable. No doors stay open as long as we might wish. Every experience comes sometimes to its end. Corridors through which we have passed are blocked off behind us. We may turn back and seem to walk there with the ghosts of memories, but we cannot walk there in fact. Faces, voices, pictures of old scenes—there they are, beckoning wistfully to our recollection; but we cannot relive the days that are gone. In the passage of time there is something ultimate. We must move on, no matter how we should like to linger, and that which was the vivid present drops into the misty past.

There is a picture in my mind which symbolizes in one small like-ness the experience that is true of all life. When I was abroad one summer, with others who were dear to me, we went at the end of our journey into the beautiful French province of Touraine to see the old chateaux. Each one of them is in charge of a guardian, and one must wait at the gate until the guardian is ready to take you with him through the castle. Into great entrances and vestibules you go, up ancient stairways, along old galleries hidden in the walls, some-times out upon turrets and parapets where the footsteps of men at arms, pacing their guard, have hollowed the gray stones, through secret rooms, into great banqueting halls. As we went, the guide would describe the history with which the particular chateau was redolent, pointing out the pictures and tapestries on the walls, the *prie-dieu* with its worn missal before which such and such a queen was wont to kneel, a chapel where hangs still the red hat of a cardinal whose life may have been mixed more strangely with dark intrigue than with religion, a room where a king held counsel with men who in other centuries were shaping the turbulent history of France. Constantly I found myself tarrying behind. There were rooms and places which I seemed never quite ready to leave, but lingered to the last moment in order that I might photograph on my mind some detail of wall or furniture or view from a mullioned window over river and park. Especially I remember standing at the end of the ascent by its superb stone staircase on the roof of the vast chateau at Chambord, and looking out in the utter quietness of that lofty place over miles and miles of the treetops of the park, drenched in the last golden radiance of a setting sun. Acutely I was conscious of a beauty that must be fleeting. Presently the sun would have gone down. Soon in any event we must leave the quiet parapet and go down the echoing, shadowed stairs. Soon we must pass out of this enchanted place also and hear the great door locked when we passed through. Day after day the same thing happened, and in that sense of an experienced beauty so vivid and yet so inevitably transient I felt then, and I perceive now, the inevitable parable of life. Constantly we pass through doors and hear them shut behind.

Yet when the doors were shut we did not come away empty. We had carried to each of those great chateaux an eagerness to see and remember all we could. In desire and imagination we had come, as it were, with lighted lamps. Therefore some of the richness of the atmosphere and the meaning of those places would belong to us always.

But sometimes the crucial fact is that our lamps have not been lighted, and so when we stand outside doors through which we cannot go again all that we can do is to be sorry for what now we cannot have. There can be in human beings like ourselves a failure to make the best of opportunity, a carelessness that does not think in time, and wakes up so late that all that is left is to knock vainly on a shut door.

There is, for example, the door of knowledge. For months and years a boy or girl has been in school. Those hours in the schoolroom, that long drudgery—as it sometimes seemed—with the book open before you on the desk, or those other hours in recitation or at the blackboard, were your open doors. You might have gone through them into mastery of what you were meant to learn. You might have entered into larger rooms of understanding and of mastery of your subjects—mathematics, science, history, literature, languages—so that they should seem to you not drudgery anymore but full of wide windows of enjoyment. But if you did not go through the doors when you had the chance, if you were lazy and indifferent, then you stand exactly where you stood before—in the midst of your own dullness, with the doors of what had been your opportunity barred against your return.

There needs to be brought into our whole educational process the serious and sobering consciousness that there are doors which, once shut, will stay shut, to our enduring loss. It is often made too easy for boys and girls to drift from stage to stage of educational advantage with little sense of penalty for failure to do their best. Many are sent to college, not because they deserve it, but because it is the expected thing, and the result is that some grow to manhood and womanhood with moral fiber which has never been made sturdy through clear distinction between a faithfulness which wins its reward because it deserves it and a faithlessness which loses its opportunity because it deserves to lose. A careless undergraduate was confronted by a more responsible friend with a question for which he had no respectable answer: "Tom, have you ever in your life done *anything* as absolutely well as you could have done it?" He knew he had not; and his resulting emptiness might be expressed in the wry sentence once spoken by President A. Lawrence Lowell, of Harvard: "It is no wonder that Harvard is such a great reservoir of learning, for the freshmen bring so much knowledge in and the seniors take so little out."

Too few in the colleges make their work a matter of conscience, or live up to the self-requirement which one of the great men of this century kept before him as written on a card upon his desk, "Do It Now."

In the biography of David Livingstone there is a revealing glimpse of the kind of education which made that boy into the man he became. "It was his father's habit to lock the door at dusk, by which time all the children were expected to be in the house. One evening David had infringed this rule, and when he reached the door it was barred. He made no cry nor disturbance, but, having procured a piece of bread, sat down contentedly to pass the night on the doorstep. There, on looking out, his mother found him."[1] Already the boy had learned that there are distinctions which may be decisive, a coming late which may be too late, and a shutting of the door which may not be lightly opened. It was because he knew this that he could move through his life's maturing purpose with such heroic and instant clearness afterward. And it is this quality which we greatly need today.

So also for the many who have gone beyond school or even college years the same essential facts are true. Here are the books open upon our tables. Here are the vital public questions daily brought before us in the newspapers, which we might have considered intelligently, and in relation to which we might have framed a living judgment. Here are the chances we have had through personal contact and discussion, or through public assemblies, to enter into the best riches of other minds. It may be we have seized these opportunities. If so, the time that has gone will have made our whole self more spacious in its thinking. But if we have not passed through the doors which long stood open, if with trivial preoccupations we have stood still in our old intellectual footprints and have played contentedly with the toys

[1] W. Garden Blaikie, *The Personal Life of David Livingstone* (New York: Fleming H. Revell, n.d.; author's Preface dated 1880), p. 26.

of our worn notions instead of pressing through to see what maturer interests lay beyond, then once more we dwell within the walls of our smallmindedness, and the doors through which we might have gone are shut.

As there is the door of knowledge, so there are the doors to what have been—or might have been—our generous activities. At any period of reckoning a man or woman may be stirred to ask, "What have I *done* that was worth doing? Here I have been in this particular community, this city, for a period of my life. Is it any better because I have lived in it?"

When religion is real it does not mean a perfunctory experience on Sundays. It means that the consciences of men and women are being made sensitive to those needs in their world which have a claim upon them as Christians. Such men and women may not seem to do anything dramatic. They will not seek recognition or reward. But they are the ones who will respond when volunteers are needed to strengthen some organization devoted to the public good: to improve the schools, to get some decent houses built instead of slums, to help the poor, to turn the light on civic corruption or neglect which the prosperous may not know of but which falls with cruel weight on the unprivileged and defenseless. At its best the Church can produce great souls, like that gallant soldier of the nineteenth century whose memorial in St. Paul's Cathedral, London, reads:

> TO CHARLES GEORGE GORDON
> WHO ALWAYS AND EVERYWHERE
> GAVE HIS STRENGTH TO THE WEAK,
> HIS SUBSTANCE TO THE POOR,
> HIS SYMPATHY TO SUFFERING,
> AND HIS HEART TO GOD.

The trouble is that men and women of that sort may be few, and there are too many—including ministers—who have been so absorbed in their narrow affairs that they have amounted to almost nothing as effective citizens. By contrast, Martin Luther King, then an unknown pastor of an obscure Negro church in Montgomery, Alabama, began to champion the cause of his people against the indignities to which they were subjected in so routine a matter as their riding on the buses when they went to work; and then little by little became the leader—through risk and danger—toward the whole larger freedom of opportunity which his people had been denied.

Meanwhile, there were white men, in and out of the churches, far more influential then than he, who did nothing. What may they have thought in later years, one wonders, when they looked at the shut doors of what could have been their opportunity and realized that the lamps of their compassionate concern had either never been lighted or at the critical moment had gone out. Concerning them there might be written what Rudyard Kipling wrote of *Tomlinson:*

> "Stand up, stand up now, Tomlinson, and answer loud and high.
> The good that ye did for the sake of men or ever ye came to die—
> The good that ye did for the sake of men in little earth so lone!"
> And the naked soul of Tomlinson grew white as a rain-washed bone!

Not only for individuals but for a whole people there can be opportunities which once neglected can be irrecoverable. At the end of the First World War, the United States listened to the cheap slogan "Back to normalcy," thought it could advance its own interests and let the rest of the world go hang, and drifted into isolationism. It turned its back on the League of Nations which might have made possible then a decent world adjustment and a stable peace, and it left the ground open for the growth of hatreds whose fruit was Hitlerism and the Second World War. Elihu Root, who had been a United States Senator and Secretary of State, said in New York in 1927, "We have allowed insensate prejudice and camouflaged but futile phrases to appear—but falsely appear—to represent the true heart of the American people, with all its idealism, with its breadth of human sympathy, with its strong desire that our country should do its share for peace and happiness and noble life in all the world." We neglected for too long the whole critical need for justice to the Negro and equal opportunity of the races here at home, and the result was the passion and violence that broke loose in Alabama and Mississippi and elsewhere in 1964. We do not always fail like that, but whenever we *are* guilty of long carelessness we stand outside shut doors of opportunity which if we can open again at all we shall open only with cost and pain.

There is a third and most poignant way in which we may stand before shut doors. It is in the stabbing realization of what we may have lost in friendship and in love because we were sometimes stupid and neglectful.

Here around us have been the hearts of little children. As you look back over the months or the years, was there a time when you said to yourself that you must come into closer contact with them: with those growing boys and girls of your own whose childishness sometimes only provoked your impatience when you knew that it ought to have called out your understanding gentleness? You said you would play with them more. You would listen with a quicker readiness to their questions. You would try to cultivate their comradeship, so that it would be instinctive for them to come to you with their confidences, and you and they would share each other's interests more and more. All that possibility stood before you, but did you enter through what then were the open doors? Or have you forgotten? Did you let the hard preoccupations of your money-getting claim you, and the tense grip of what you thought were "practical duties" hold you, so that you appeared to have no time for the sympathies which require the outgoing mind at leisure from itself? If so, you may be feeling what one man wrote to a friend: "Just recently I became aware of my own sinfulness in failing to recognize how much there is to be thankful for; failure to *appreciate* my children being a flagrant example." If so, also, you may be paying now a bitter price. Those who were the little boys and girls but have grown up now through adolescence may have moved beyond your reach. Little by little you have built up in them a wall of disappointment which you cannot readily get through. "He never took the trouble to try to understand us," they may be saying. "We wanted him, but he was so busy with something else or so forgetful that he did not come."

So it may happen also with the most intimate and sacred relationship of all, the relationship of a husband and a wife. Some marriages are broken by positive unfaithfulness and overt cruelty. But many which are never formally broken may nevertheless have all their substance turned to dust by a slow withering of the love that once was there. A husband did not mean to let his wife imagine that she is not dear to him, but he has forgotten the little things that would have made her know that she was and is: the word of appreciation, the eyes looking into her eyes, the quiet moments sharing with her what is deepest in his mind and heart. Therefore the time comes when small threads of gradual alienation have thickened into a veil between them, so that they move on the two sides of it with no sure touch between. Then one may say, "If only I had thought in time! If only I could go back and live the years again, how much more imaginative I might have been for the words and acts that express devotion and could have kept the comradeship of mind and heart complete! If only I had remembered soon enough, and not let the lamps go out!" But some of them did go out; and so when one would find his way again into the largeness of life to which he had been invited, he finds to his desolation that the door is shut.

II

Such then would seem to be the message of the parable. But it would be a dreadful thing if in all instances of our foolishness and our failure "the door was shut" had to be the final word. For *some* opportunities it *will* be the final word; no presumptuous carelessness can cover up that fact. But our hope is that there is an everlasting mercy which can show to our awakened selves a new way ahead, and so not leave us to be judged alone for the way which at first we did not follow. In the Book of Revelation there is a promise which the heart reaches out to trust in. "Behold, I have set before you an open door, which no man can shut." Because the spirit of God in Christ is patient beyond our deserving, there may come to those who have been careless and casual some fresh inspiration which will light the lamps that had gone out, and guide our steps this time to an open door.

This new inspiration may come through some other person who is made in this respect to be an instrument of God. Here, for example, are young people in school or college who thus far have had no keen desire for knowledge or achievement, and so they have sat down and gone to sleep. Then some sudden influence stabs them wide awake: the provocation of an exciting teacher, the sharp rebuke of a candid friend, the shaming realization that while they might be moving ahead in intelligence and efficiency they are on a dead-end street. They cannot make up for the carelessness of the days that have been wasted, but they can keep from wasting any more. So the girl who has been frivolous begins to see the larger dimensions of herself, and moves forward toward the fullness of her womanhood. So the boy who has heretofore done nothing starts trying to do his best. Finished with college and caught now by a positive purpose which takes him toward the hard training of engineering or scientific research, of law or medicine or the ministry, he is a different person. He will not again be so neglectful of opportunity as to be found standing outside doors that have been shut.

It is a blessing to any man if he has someone who will tell him the truth about himself in time. Lyndon B. Johnson, President of the United States, might not have had any notable career if it had not been for his mother. As he told the writer of a magazine article in

1965, "I'd probably have been a school drop-out and never even have finished high school if she hadn't kept after me. She kept working on me to better myself. I remember her, many mornings, following me down to the ranch gate, a book in her hand, to be sure that I passed a test." When he did graduate from high school, he rebelled against any more schooling; and for two years he was a pick-and-shovel man, working on the county road. "I'd still be there," he said, "working on some road, or maybe driving a truck, if it weren't for my mother." One Sunday morning when he had been sleeping late, his mother came into his room just as he woke up. "She sat on the foot of the bed," he remembered, "and there was a sad look on her face. 'I never thought my first-born would be content just to be a road-hand,' she said. It hurt me, and I said all right, I'd go to college."[2] He told his mother that he didn't know whether he could work with his brains, but he was ready to try. He did get into college, with a loan his mother managed; and beginning with that day, what might have been a neglected door opened before him upon a long way ahead.

It was through another person that a great man of the century before this one was also helped to find his open door. Phillips Brooks, after he had graduated from Harvard in 1855 when he was not yet twenty years old, was given a position as a teacher in the Boston Latin School. Too young and unprepared to handle a class of turbulent boys in a school run by a headmaster who believed in rough methods, he was dismissed by that headmaster as an ignominious failure. "I don't know what will become of me," he wrote; "I don't seem in the way to come to much now." In his own eyes, and in the eyes of many of his friends, there seemed to be no promising future for him. But one day he talked with Dr. Walker, the president of Harvard, of whom it was said that he was "a veritable confessor of souls by an inward divine appointment"; and Dr. Walker told him that his place was in the ministry. "He had discarded ambition," wrote his biographer, Alexander A. G. Allen, "and was willing to be no one; he only asked to be useful."[3] Hesitantly then Phillips Brooks entered the Virginia Seminary. "He had a misgiving that his years at Harvard had not been improved to the utmost," and "he made a determination to do hard and thorough work."[4] Also there was

---

[2] Isabelle Shelton, "Lyndon Johnson's Mother," *Saturday Evening Post*, May 8, 1965.

[3] *Life and Letters of Phillips Brooks*, Vol. I (New York: E. P. Dutton & Co., 1901), p. 147.

[4] *Ibid.*, p. 178.

"ripening within him the consciousness that he was called by God, and that in this conviction he could not be lessened or restricted."[5] So instead of the door which had been shut before him, there opened a new and larger door, through which he went to a wideness of understanding and of service such as few in his generation could achieve.

Thus in the area of outward achievement the grace of God may give us a second chance. But what of the inner life, that is most precious? If the doors to which we have come too late are those which would have opened into a comradeship and love that we neglected, what then? How can any remorse of ours change the fact that now we stand outside?

No, nothing that we say or feel can be enough. We dare not think that when, through our neglect, the door has been shut we have any right to knock and demand that it be opened. Not from our side now can any initiative proceed. But the redeeming fact is that from the other side the undeserved mercy may come—as though in the parable the bridegroom himself had opened the shut door and found his way to those who had let their lamps go out and lifted them up to follow him. That is the everlasting meaning of the atonement: a compassion in the heart of God that cannot rest when even the unworthy are left outside. So the promise, "Behold, I have set before you an open door which no man can shut" may mean that not even our failures and sins can keep the door shut against the divine mercy that chooses to come through. So it was with Jesus. So it may be with the human souls that reflect what was in him. When love has waited for us and we have not come, it has its own sorrow for the part of life that has been lost, but that sorrow is forever ready to be redeeming. "Love bears all things, believes all things, hopes all things, endures all things. Love never ends." Therefore if we have deeply learned our need, and our hearts are desolate as we stand outside the door, we may dare to cry to the human love which is the embodiment of the love of God: "Let it even now be not too late. Unworthy as I am, open the door which my stupidity might have caused to be closed completely, and let my chastened soul come in!"

5 *Ibid.,* p. 147.

14.

The Man Who Enlarged Other Men

He was a good man, full of the Holy
Spirit and of faith.

ACTS 11:24

THE MAN spoken of was Barnabas. In the calendar of the Church
year as contained in the Book of Common Prayer there are days set
apart for commemoration of the great figures of the early Church.
Except for the twelve disciples (minus Judas) whom Jesus first chose
to be with him and Matthias chosen later to complete the twelve, the
Evangelists and Paul, Barnabas is the only one included in the list.

Why? He was not as conspicuous as some of the others. Peter was
more aggressive and commanding. John had a special relationship to
Jesus which Barnabas never had. Paul was incomparably a greater
thinker. But Barnabas brings to ordinary would-be Christians a kind
of inspiration which not many of the others can convey. His eminence
was not that of a genius, but that of the man who takes endowments
not outstandingly different from those of the average man and makes
nobility out of them. He was not thinking much of himself or trying
to be great. He simply let God use him whenever the chance came to
help somebody else; and in helping others to be better than they
would have been without him, the Spirit of God wrought in him the
greatness that he did not seek.

I

There is no long account of Barnabas anywhere in the New Testament, but the references to him are sufficiently vivid to make his
figure clear.

He is introduced first as "Joseph, a Levite, a native of Cyprus."
The fact that he was a Levite meant that he was part of the eccle-

siastical establishment, and *might* have meant that he was a man of conventional ideas and narrow sympathies. But the direct opposite was true. He was concerned for other people and for what might be their needs. The first thing we know of that he did was to sell some land he had, bring the money to Peter and the other apostles, and ask them to use it for the poor.

The next we hear of him is in connection with the great personality in whose life he was to play a crucial part. Saul, the fanatical Pharisee, who regarded the followers of Jesus as blasphemous subverters of Judaism, and now was armed with a commission to arrest any of those followers he could lay hands on, was on his way from Jerusalem to Damascus. On his journey, with shattering suddenness, he had a vision of the risen Christ which turned his whole life upside down. From that moment he would dedicate himself to be the evangelist of that which he had persecuted. In Damascus he declared his new loyalty, to the anger and consternation of the synagogues. Later, he went back to Jerusalem, that he might tell all the fellowship of Jesus there of his change of heart.

But what he met with was disbelief. Saul the persecutor converted, this same Saul whose name had been a word of terror—who could take the risk of believing that? Was the wolf any less the wolf for coming now in sheep's clothing? What might he have in mind except a treacherous stratagem by which to find out more surely who the disciples of Jesus were? So the little company in Jerusalem wanted no contact with him. Let him keep his distance. Who could trust anything he had to say?

Thus it might have come to pass that the man destined to become the greatest apostle of Christianity would instead have been rejected—and would have been, except for Barnabas. Barnabas sponsored Saul, and persuaded the others in Jerusalem to take him in.

After a time, Paul—as his name now had been changed to be—goes away to Tarsus, his native city, while Barnabas remains in Jerusalem. He stays there while many are scattered by a persecution which broke out against all those who were disciples of Christ. Then there comes the report that by the witness of some of these disciples, who had got as far as Antioch, many persons in that great city had been converted. The church in Jerusalem sends Barnabas to Antioch to learn exactly what had happened; and when he arrives there he discovers that among those who had been converted were Gentiles as well as Jews. So "when he saw the grace of God, he was glad, and he exhorted them all to remain faithful to the Lord with steadfast purpose." And it is at this point in the narrative of the Book of Acts that there comes the description of Barnabas himself, "a good man, full of the Holy Spirit and of faith."

As Barnabas "was glad" when he saw what the grace of God had begun to do in Antioch, so his faith reached out to follow what it might do further. He remembered Paul, and off he went to Tarsus to persuade Paul to come to Antioch. Paul did come with him—and there in Antioch the followers of Jesus were first called Christians. And the first thing that this little Christian company did was to show that it was concerned with something larger than itself. It might have said to Paul and Barnabas, "Stay here. *We* need you." Instead of that, by an action which spoke louder than words, it said, "People everywhere need you. Go carry the gospel of Christ to some of those who have never heard it." So, after they had laid hands on Paul and Barnabas in benediction, they sent them off by ship to Cyprus. From there the two sailed again to the mainland of Asia Minor and began the missionary journey the exciting story of which—with its hazards and hardships and also its rich results—is told of in chapters 13 and 14 of the Book of Acts.

Thus far the careers of Barnabas and Paul moved together. Then there came a separation that was to reveal—as we shall see—which man had the surer insight. At the end of the first missionary journey the two of them went up to Jerusalem to tell the church there what had happened, and to plead for a liberty of Christian evangelism which would admit Gentiles as well as Jews into the Church of Jesus. After that they were ready to start out again. "Let us return and visit the brethren in every city where we proclaimed the word of the Lord, and see how they are," said Paul. And they would take John Mark with them, said Barnabas. No, they would not, said Paul. For John Mark had been with them on the first journey, at the beginning of it; then, because he was afraid, or for some other hidden reason, he left them and turned back. Barnabas wanted to trust him again; but not Paul. The disagreement was so sharp that they went their separate ways. Paul took a man named Silas as his companion and went again to Asia Minor. Barnabas took Mark and went to Cyprus.

That is the last time Barnabas' name appears in the Book of Acts. But there is one other previous reference to him which needs to be remembered. When he and Paul were preaching in the city of Lystra on their journey together, the crowd was so excited by what these two men said and did that some shouted out, "The gods have come down to us in the likeness of men!" Because Paul was the chief speaker, they said he must be Hermes, but Barnabas they called Zeus. A large man, therefore, and majestic of person he must have been, and the look of him was a fitting index for all that we have already seen his character to represent. There was something about him which is best described as bigness. As he was big framed, so he was big hearted. He was one of those magnanimous, generous spirits who make life seem to all men the more worth living when they have come into contact with that glowing strength.

II

Review, then, those incidents in which we have seen him, and mark how this impression of Barnabas is consistent throughout. The first mention of him had to do—as we remembered—with an act of exceptional generosity. The fact that there were many poor people in Jerusalem meant to Barnabas the blessedness of giving to others for his Master's sake. So he sold the piece of land which he had and gave the proceeds to the apostles for relief in the church. He would take his personal property and use it to enrich the life of the whole body.

Mark him, too, as he goes forward to welcome Saul when Saul comes up to Jerusalem. There is no record that he had ever seen Saul in any other aspect than that in which the rest of the Christians had seen him. To him also Saul had been known previously as the dreaded persecutor. He had no better evidence than the others that Saul had actually been converted into the disciple Paul, as he now called himself. But there was an outgoing warmth of trust in Barnabas which made him the first to believe in the possibilities of Paul's new discipleship, and he committed himself to that belief while all the rest were timid and uncertain.

Consider also the spirit of Barnabas when, later on, he was sent to Antioch to follow up the report that a new little Christian fellowship was developing there. Barnabas found that to be excitingly true. The gospel was reaching out now not only to Jews but to Gentiles also. Another man might conceivably have wished to stay there alone and win for himself the credit for what was beginning to happen. But Barnabas had none of the smallness of spirit which might appropriate an opportunity for his own. He went off at once to seek Paul, the abler man; the man who was at length to overshadow him in service for the Church. He brought Paul to Antioch and served with him wholeheartedly there. He went with Paul on their joint missionary venture to Asia Minor, and stood shoulder to shoulder with Paul when they went together afterward to plead the cause of the Gentiles before the Council of the church at Jerusalem. And when at last he separated from Paul, it was for no personal reason, but only that he might do for another exactly what he had once done for Paul himself: welcome, strengthen and save from frustration a man who stood under suspicion and was in danger of being condemned. The young John Mark who had started with Paul and himself on the first missionary journey and then had turned back—what about him when a second journey was proposed? Paul would have no more of Mark. Once a man had been a failure, let him stay a failure. But Barnabas had a more generous trust. At whatever risk, he would give Mark another chance. And it was Barnabas, not Paul, who proved to be right. Without Barnabas, Mark might have drifted out into the gray company of the lost and abandoned men. But Barnabas saved him—saved him to become the writer of the Gospel which stands second in our New Testament but actually was the first one written; saved him to become the man about whom Paul himself years later, when he was a prisoner in Rome, wrote in a letter to his beloved Timothy, "Get Mark and bring him with you, for he is very useful in serving me."

If now we should seek for one short phrase which would express the character of Barnabas we can find it at the end of the first passage in the Book of Acts that refers to him. He was "Joseph, a Levite." That was his actual own name. But that was not the name by which he would afterward be called. The new name, Barnabas, by which we know him was given to him afterward by the Christian Church, to express the disciples' recognition of the kind of man he had shown himself to be. And what does Barnabas mean? It means "son of encouragement." Barnabas was the man who put new heart in everybody.

III

Who can measure, in every aspect of the world's life, the value of the man who can do that? Up to the time of the beginning of the Second World War, and for a while after that beginning, the name of Winston Churchill woke only a mixed response in the mind of the British people. He had had an up-and-down career. But in its darkest hour Great Britain turned to him: turned to him because it found in him the indomitable courage by which alone the nation could be saved. No disaster could dismay him. The near-destruction of the British army at Dunkirk was turned into a rescue so heroic that it lit a blazing torch of confidence that nothing would be impossible. And by his magnificent speeches in the House of Commons, which echoed round the world, Winston Churchill sounded the victorious trumpets to which free men everywhere responded.

When a man brings creative courage, he brings it not out of his isolated self. He brings it out of something deeper and more mighty, out of faith in some reality too eternal to be destroyed. It may be the faith of patriotism, in the grandeur of a people's destiny. It may be faith in a cause so right, so surely rooted in the truth of things, that no hazard and no darkness can keep it from prevailing. At its highest it is faith in the invincible grace of God.

That was the sort of faith Barnabas had, faith in the illimitable possibilities of God's achievements, and therefore faith in events and faith in man. The reason was that he was not only a good man; he was also "full of the Holy Spirit." There are other men always who may be called good, but whose goodness does not have any power of encouragement. They are not full of anything. No great energies flow out from them, any more than energy can flow out from a sheltered pond. Their possibilities lie like stranded vessels on the flats of inland bays, with no channels opened toward the sea horizon from whence the rush of releasing waters might pour in. But the great souls, the souls which like Barnabas bring to the lives of others the lift of a new encouragement, are those which have widened the sluices through which the ocean tides of God come in. They may not in themselves have been different from other men and women, they may not have had originally any extraordinary nature or spiritual capacity, but they have waited on the Lord. They have prayed, they have hoped, they have desired. They have let themselves be receptive to the vast inflow of the spiritual world. So they have been filled with the Holy Spirit, and out of that fullness they can let loose into other lives great currents of faith and trust by which others are redeemed.

When any life meets with no high expectation, it can become flat and meaningless. Too many influences in our world tend to create exactly that result. William E. Hocking, the philosopher, wrote once of what he considered to be the chief defect of modern education, which sometimes transmits great stores of information like a delivery of dry firewood but brings with it no inspiring purpose to kindle it into flame. So it may produce dull souls, gray and incapable of greatness, not because of lack of original endowments but "because they have never been exposed to what is noble, generous, and faith-provoking." But when any person *is* exposed to what is faith-provoking, then large consequences may follow. Herman Hagedorn, who later was to achieve literary distinction, was invited early in his career to write a biography of Theodore Roosevelt. He shrank from the suggestion as being beyond his powers. But Roosevelt said to him, "Of course you can do it. I am sure of it." When Hagedorn still demurred, Roosevelt sent him to Ripley Hitchcock, editor of *Harper's,* who would be the publisher. And when that wise and kindly man had talked with him, Hagedorn changed his mind. He would try to do what he had been stirred to believe that he might do. That meeting, he wrote afterward, "set a new course for my life."[1]

What encouragement can do is still more notably exemplified in another and earlier instance. In 1885 there came to London a young man who seemed marked for nothingness. The son of a physician, he had been sent by his father to medical school. For six years he only pretended to study and failed every examination, until the father lost hope and patience, and the son disappeared from home, a fugitive, and—as he wrote later—"without hope, in the desperate spirit of an *enfant terrible.*"[2] For three stark years he drifted in the submerged wretchedness of the down-and-outs of London, picking up a few pennies from selling matches, from holding horses or from begging; eating remnants from vegetable wagons, shivering under newspapers at night in doorways and alleys. On scraps of torn paper he had begun to write verse, and once he mailed something he had written to Wilfrid Meynell, the editor of the magazine *Merry England.* For six months the grubby unsolicited manuscript lay unread in the magazine's office. Then Meynell saw it. Impressed, he sent a letter to the Charing Cross post office, the only address the manuscript had borne, and his letter was returned unclaimed. Then a strange series of accidents brought the writer of the manuscript to Meynell's door—ragged, destitute, despairing. Meynell not only gave him a check for what he had written. He got him clothes. He sent him to a physician. He took him for a while into his own house. He made him believe that he could be a poet. And this derelict whom Meynell rescued was Francis Thompson, who would write *The Hound of Heaven.*

Who is there of us that cannot remember some way and some time—or many a time—when life has been made different by an encouraging word? It may have been the word of a teacher, holding us to high standards and summoning up courage to face some task we were about to abandon. It may have been the word of some older man in his profession who took notice of us when we thought that there was nothing in us to deserve his recognition. But more important are the lovely intimate encouragements which come to us from those who are closest to our life: a mother's trust in her son, a

[1] Herman Hagedorn, *The Hyphenated Family* (New York: The Macmillan Company, 1960) pp. 239, 240.

[2] J. C. Reid, *Francis Thompson, Man and Poet* (London: Routledge and Kegan Paul, 1959), p. 24.

wife's unfaltering loyalty to the man she has married and who by her devotion is made better than without her he ever could have been.

In the great issues of our whole world's life also there is need of the encouraging voice. At the beginning of this century there was confidence—though a shallow and mistaken confidence—that all was going well with mankind. The general expectation was that human contrivance had built a world order which guaranteed smooth progress for the years ahead. The tide of bland assurance was at the full. Then came the appalling disillusionment of the two world wars, and with it a complete reversal of the prevailing mood. A gray cynicism began to creep into the common mind, and it was reflected in theology. Instead of belief in human possibilities there came increasing emphasis on human depravity, and the sound of iron bells that prophesied impending doom. Instead of the high tide of confidence, one could only hear

> Its melancholy, long, withdrawing roar,
> Retreating, to the breath
> Of the night wind, down the vast edges drear
> And naked shingles of the world.[3]

Insofar as that mood prevails, there can come paralysis of hopeful and creative energies. Men could be misled into saying of all idealistic efforts: What's the use? Human nature is too much the slave of its passions, the blind self-absorption of individuals and nations too inveterate for there to be any hope of building a better world. Forget about the United Nations, just as America forgot about the League before, and helped destroy it. Count all far-reaching purposes, whether of the individual or of society, as futile; and echo the mordant words of Theodore Dreiser:

Life is to me too much of a welter and play of inscrutable forces to permit any significant comment. . . . The unutterably infinitesimal individual weaves among the mysteries a floss-like and wholly meaningless course— if course it be. In short, I catch no meaning from all I have seen and pass quite as I came, confused and dismayed.[4]

What can save us from the futility of that despair? The rising up in our world of men like Barnabas; the coming of those who like him can be sons of encouragement; the emergence of souls who possess

---

[3] Matthew Arnold, *Dover Beach.*
[4] *Living Philosophies* (New York: Simon and Schuster, 1931), p. 14.

the positive and invincible goodness which springs from being filled
with the Holy Spirit and therefore being full of faith!

"No Time need have gone to ruin," wrote Thomas Carlyle in
Heroes and Hero-Worship, "could it have found a man great enough,
a man wise and good enough; wisdom to discern truly what the Time
wanted, valour to lead it on the right road thither; these are the salvation of any Time. But I liken common languid Times, with their
unbelief, distress, perplexity, with their doubting characters and
embarrassed circumstances, impotently crumbling down into ever
worse distress towards final ruin;—all this I liken to dry dead fuel,
waiting for the lightning out of Heaven that shall kindle it. The great
man, with his free force direct out of God's own hand, is the lightning.
His word is the wise healing word which all can believe in. All
blazes round him, when he has once struck on it, into fire like his
own."

Such men more than once have shaped the course of history, and
can shape it now. Barnabas turned it in a new direction when his
brave faith recognized the giant possibilities in Paul, and when the two
together dared to go out to carry the Christian gospel to the whole
Roman world. Martin Luther changed it when he dared confront his
world in the power that comes to a single soul, once the Holy Spirit
has possessed it. Woodrow Wilson, the first American statesman who
appreciated the new sweep of world events and the imperative need
for world cooperation if humanity is not to be destroyed, seemed to
fail; but beyond temporary failure, the great truth re-emerges as an
inextinguishable light. In most governments, and among the common
people, men of any sanity are recognizing that there has got to be a
different world if any world at all and any decent human life upon
it are to continue to exist. Old hatreds and suspicions, and the insensate passions that lead to war, die hard. Only by great and steady
faith can they be overcome, faith that burned in such men as Dag
Hammarskjöld and Adlai Stevenson, and in others who come to the
dispirited with the saving strength of their encouragement.

Of such a spirit Walter Lippmann wrote in 1963 in a tribute which
he entitled "The Miracle of Pope John."

It is a modern miracle that anyone should reach across all the barriers
of class, caste, color and creed to touch the hearts of all kinds of people.
. . . That they have responded is proof that the enmities and divisions of
mankind are not the whole reality of the human condition. There is in
men a capacity, unplumbed and perhaps unmeasurable, to be reached by
loving kindness. . . . We know that the miracle of Pope John will not

transform the world. . . . We shall not suddenly become new men. But the universal response which Pope John evoked is witness to the truth that there is in the human person, however prone to evil, an aptitude for goodness. That is why we must never despair that the world can be better than the world we live in.[5]

Thank God then for the Barnabas souls, with their gallant goodness and their faith in goodness, who have touched our own lives with their uplifting trust! And pray that something of their same spirit may be in us, that we may bring to others the confidence which shall make them go more bravely on their way.

[5] *Washington Post,* June 6, 1963.

15.

The Man Who Lost His Opportunity

And as he argued about justice and self-control
and future judgment, Felix was alarmed and
said, "Go away for the present; when I have an
opportunity I will summon you."

ACTS 24:25

ONE OF the great sources of the power of the Bible is that it is so graphic. It does not deal with abstractions. It reveals truth through persons. Again and again in its pages one stands in the presence of dramatic confrontations: Joseph and his brothers, Moses and Pharaoh, Nathan and David, Elijah and Ahab. And here is another: Paul the apostle of Jesus Christ, and Felix, the Roman governor, in Caesarea.

It is near the end of Paul's career. In one of his letters to the church at Corinth he had summed up what life had brought him: "afflictions, hardships, calamities, beatings, imprisonments, tumults." He had just been in mortal peril from a screaming mob at the Temple in Jerusalem, and might have been killed except for the intervention of the tribune commanding the armed guard. He had been taken under protective custody to Caesarea to await examination. He was alone and unfriended. In that bleak situation it seemed that he had nothing to depend on. Outwardly he did not. But he had something within that the eyes of others could not see: "the power of God, the weapons of righteousness," and the knowledge his long dedication had given him that "having nothing" he was "yet possessing every thing."

Now he stands before a Roman governor who had all the consequence which he appeared to lack. He was the one on trial. Such was the fact that every obvious circumstance would indicate. But in the long light of history it would be the Roman, not Paul, who stood there to be tried—and judged.

His name was Antonius Felix. His brother had stood high in the favor of the Emperor Claudius, and because of that relationship Claudius had made Antonius Felix procurator of Palestine in A.D. 52. He had been three times married, the last time to the young and beautiful Drusilla, the daughter of Herod Agrippa I. She had been married before, although little more than a child, to the king of Emesa, and Felix, when he came into the province, had seen her and determined to possess her. Therefore, through evil influences he drew her away from her husband, and married her himself. His administration was a turbulent one. A man of strong passions, ruthless and tyrannous, he exercised his authority with a cynical contempt for life and liberty. His was not a judgment seat before which one would have chosen to appear. Yet even in this man, corrupt and passionate, there were the glimmerings of a conscience which had not been quite destroyed. He was perhaps not worse than other officials of his time, but neither was he better. He belonged to his world in the sense of accepting its prevailing values, and had no strong desire to rise above it. He would not have readily understood the words which Paul had written to one of his churches, "Do not be conformed to this world, but be transformed by the renewal of your mind." In that fact he was typical of many men before and since: men not conspicuously evil, but men whose failure is that they take things as they are, accept the crowd's standards as being good enough, and have no awakening spirit that would make them see that there is a world of higher meanings which could illumine the common world in which they move.

I

Note first the attitude which Felix took toward the charges made against Paul.

When Paul was brought to Caesarea by the escort sent by Lysias, the tribune in Jerusalem, the escort delivered to Felix a letter from Lysias telling why Paul had been taken into custody, and outlining the charges made against him by the Jewish authorities in Jerusalem. "I will hear you when your accusers arrive," said Felix, and he kept Paul guarded. Then after five days the accusers came, headed by the high priest and by a spokesman named Tertullus. They arraigned Paul on three counts. They said, in the first place, that he was "a pestilent fellow, an agitator among the Jews throughout the world"; and in the second place, "a ring-leader of the sect of the Nazarenes." In the third place, that "he even tried to profane the temple," because he brought Gentiles with him into it. In other words, they accused him of conspiracy, of religious heresy, and of irreverence for Jewish traditions.

These charges doubtless made very different impressions on the Roman's mind. To the first he would be instantly alert. There was nothing that the Roman guardians of the provinces watched for with more immediate and grim jealousy than any sign of rebellion. They were swift to crush it when they believed it to exist. Neither did they dare ignore a charge of it even when they suspected that the charge was false. There was danger always that hostile influences might accuse them to the high powers in Rome of disaffection, if their authority relaxed its harshness. Pilate had been intimidated by the cry of the Jewish mob. "If you release this man, you are not Caesar's friend!" Felix, similarly, knew that when Paul was accused of sedition he might not easily dismiss the case.

As to the other two charges, the Roman, in all probability, listened to them with ill-concealed contempt. What were they—all these pestilent Jews—but squabbling sects who contended fiercely about empty superstitions? There was a kind of worship which he knew and did not disregard. It was the worship of that power which was expressed in the greatness of the empire—the worship that builded its temples to the spirit of Rome, and put the busts of the emperors in them as symbols of a deity that the legions had proved and the tax-gathers had turned into profit. In that school of religion he was an apt pupil: in that calculating worship of this world in which flattery and subservient obedience and shrewd self-seeking are the accepted homage, and power and wealth and promotion the tangible rewards. But the unprofitable religion of this conquered province, with its priests and its sacrifices and its incomprehensible ritual, the Roman regarded with a cool disdain. And as for the profaning of the Temple, of which they accused Paul, little did he concern himself with that either. To his mind this whole matter was like so much solemn chatter over nothing.

Yet what was it, as a matter of fact, that he was called upon to decide? Here, on the one hand, were the spokesmen of a religion which in its deepest fact was full of meaning and of ancient grandeur: a religion whose eternal message had been spoken by prophets whose voices had begun to sound in Palestine a hundred years before Rome was born. The religion for which they spoke carried in its heart the hopes and dreams of the noblest spirits of many centuries. It was true that these men who stood before Felix were poor representatives of so great a heritage. These smirking priests, this glib Tertullus, did not convey a sense of the spiritual passion of that worship of

Israel which they claimed to defend. Yet behind these men there did lie a reality, hidden from the Roman's eyes, which a greater man might have recognized.

And, at the same time, there stood before him the figure in whom even Felix ought to have seen the greatness. Here was a man who represented in himself the flaming passion of a new and overcoming faith. Here was one who had gathered into his soul all that was best and purest of the religion of Israel, and had set that, like a halo, round the head of the divine Master whom he proclaimed. Here was one whose religion, and whose life, had shown the power of God come down into the world of men.

Yet it was all lost upon Felix. He had no conception of the real issues which were there at stake. Like a deaf man in the presence of music, he saw only a hollow pantomime, where a greater soul might have heard the mighty surgings of the thoughts of God.

And thus it is with that spirit of the world which Felix incarnated. That spirit clothed itself long ago in the person of the Roman governor. It may clothe itself in other forms in every generation. It does not always choose for its embodiment corrupt men like Felix. It may express itself in men who in their own personal moral life are irreproachable—men against whom no public accusation can be brought. Yet they, nevertheless, may have the same indifference to the things of the spirit.

The mark of such men is that they cannot recognize the realities which are invisible to the eyes of the flesh. They can understand well enough what they can weigh in the world's balances and put into a bank account. They know what pays off in the currency of popular opinion. They are experts—or think they are—in what they consider to be practical affairs. But they may look half with amusement and half with suspicion upon any who would intrude their inconvenient ideal notions into the status quo.

"Half with amusement," we said first. As Felix listened to Tertullus, and afterward listened to Paul, he may have asked himself, "What are all these tiresome arguments about?" In every period, the man like Felix observes the disputes, the controversies, even the wranglings, which may mark some among the divided elements of those who claim alike to be worshiping God. But he has no eye to see the deeper and undergirding reality. Because he hears some things said in the name of religion which are obviously shallow and foolish, he proceeds to his own equally shallow and foolish conclusion that all that can be said of religion is likewise shallow and trivial. He assumes—as Felix did—an attitude of indifferent superiority. He thinks that his own shrewd common sense has nothing to do with such thin vagaries. Let the Church go on its way, and have its prayers and its services and its creeds, if it will. These things are all very well for those who choose to believe in them, but the sensible man of the world is too much occupied, so he thinks, with practical matters, to concern himself with such uncertain speculations. So he stands aloof and does not realize that he has suffered any loss.

But it often happens that the worldly minded man's amusement changes to something very different: to suspicion and hostility. As long as the Church and religion in general keep to an abstract worship which can be safely ignored because it has no relevance to everyday affairs, he and his associates will speak of religion with politeness and even with flattery. "Of course every community ought to have churches in it. It would hardly be respectable without them." But let religious leaders begin to question the accepted order. Let them join a protest against some old evil—entrenched landlordism which maintains profitable rotten tenements where the poor are forced to live, starvation pay to migrants brought in to work on farms, racial discrimination—and the man whose chief interest is altogether selfish will quickly change from his bland unconcern. He wants nobody to start any disturbing ideas that would interfere with "what is necessary for prosperity." The would-be reformer of even some obvious social or economic outrage may be denounced as what Paul was accused of being, "a pestilent fellow, an agitator." The vested interests may begin to say, "Let's get rid of him."

II

We pass on to note a second thing which we may mark in the spirit of Felix. If the first reason why he was indifferent to the great meaning that might have shone for him as Paul stood before him was because the spirit of his world had made him dull to values higher than those of common thinking, the second reason was because his mind was biased by the sense of power.

He was a representative of the supreme authority of his time. Behind him was all the force of the legions which had subjugated the world. In his decision was the weight of the awful name of Rome. Upon that judgment seat of his he felt the intoxication of this mighty system of which he was a part. He was the master to whom these people who came to his hall were suppliants. He was great, and they were small.

So, when one day, accompanied by a note from the centurion at

Jerusalem, there came to him at Caesarea a certain Jew—small of stature, emaciated by the hardships which he had undergone by land and sea, scarred, perhaps, even at that moment, by the violence of the mob in the Temple courts—little likelihood was there that Felix should see in him aught but an inferior. Certainly this prisoner had no outward authority about him. He had no prestige or influential friends. He stood alone against powerful public opinion. He had no greatness about him save the greatness of his soul within. And *that* the eyes of Felix could not see.

Is there not here a picture of the likelihood that always exists? Who does not know, as he looks at the life around him, and perhaps looks at his own thoughts, that the greatness and authority which are of this world tend to look down upon all who are not clothed with adventitious dignities? It is hard for the man of wealth to think that the poor man is as much of a personage as himself. He has had the power and the energy to achieve obvious results—to beat down difficulties, to pass by lesser rivals, to grasp the prize that many sought for and he alone attained. The poor man, in contrast, seems to have got but little of what the world calls success. So the man of wealth, in spite of his outward courtesy, inwardly regards him with a sort of tolerant condescension.

Now it may be true that the seeming is also the reality. It may be true that the poor man is an inferior man to the wealthy and powerful one, because he may merely have been one who sought the same things that the strong man fought for, but sought only with a weaker will and a flagging endeavor which spelled defeat. Yet, on the other hand, it may be true that the man who in the outward accounting seems to be inferior is the greater of the two. The reason why he never attained wealth may be because he would not make the sacrifice of character which in his circumstances would have been required to get it. He may have had the courage to seem to fail in material self-seeking, while the other man was the slave of his own ambitions and the coward who bent to the expectations of the crowd. He may be one who holds within himself a light beside which the tinsel glitter of the rich man's trappings are cheap and mean. Yet, nonetheless, the spirit of the world may account this man the lesser of the two because its infatuation with what it calls success cannot understand an eminence which does not stand upon a pedestal like its own. So the office holder may look down upon the man of larger soul whom he, through some shallow appeal, has defeated. So the orator who gets the plaudits of the crowd may plume himself above the calm, still speaker of the truth from whom the populace turn away. So the sleek priest Amaziah despises the unflinching message of the prophet Amos, so a Belshazzar condemns a Daniel, so a puppet upon the papal throne, Leo X, hurls his excommunications against a Martin Luther; and so the Roman Felix, puffed up with his own importance, sees only an insignificant pleader in the person of the Apostle Paul.

In the truth of God there are strange reversals. "Behold, I say to you, the first shall be last and the last first." If the shallow judgments of the world are not to lead us far astray in the very moment when we seem to feel most our success and our achievement, let us remember and guard against this perilous spirit which in the pride of its own worldliness fails to see the grandeur of those spiritual influences which may move through the world in humble garb.

III

The third phase of Felix's relationship to Paul brings in a sordid element. "He sent for him often and conversed with him," says the narrative in the Book of Acts. Why was this? Does it mean that Felix had begun to be genuinely impressed by the character of this man before him? Does it mean that he is seeking light and guidance for a troubled spirit? No. Listen to the ugly contradiction. "He hoped that money would be given him by Paul." In other words, he had slid down to that low level of meanness where all the authority and prestige of his position was mixed up for him with a hungry appetite for graft.

Is that spirit of Felix quite as exceptional as we should like to think it to be? Circumstances do not usually shape themselves in such wise as to make the matter so glaring as it was in his case. But often it is true, nonetheless, that the worldly minded man may determine his relationship to religion in terms of "What do I get out of it?" "If you will pay my price," it says in effect as Felix said to Paul, "I will advance your interests." Here, for example, is some city organization founded to help the poor. As long as it doles out individual relief, no one will object to it. But suppose it begins to ask *why* so many people are on relief, and finds that the answer lies in low wages, extortionate rents, and the mass helplessness of workers caught in the grip of economic interests they cannot resist. And suppose that the Charity Organization Society—to use a name that once was familiar—decides that its business ought to be something bigger than distributing charity; ought to be, instead, a public revelation of the oppressive forces which are keeping too many people poor. Then

men like Felix will be quick with their demand: "Stop that inter-
ference in matters where we are making profits." They are not
asking that they be *given* money, as was the case between Felix
and Paul. The situation is not so crude as that. But they *are* demanding that nobody interfere with the accustomed ways in which they
are *making* money. And if any disturbing persons will not come to
heel, then so much the worse for them—as Felix could make things
worse for Paul.

Or suppose some minister in a church whose knowledge has been
wakened and his conscience stirred by some specific social wrong in
his community begins to challenge this in the name of the gospel of
Christ. As long as things have gone on placidly and no disturbing
word has come from the pulpit, well-to-do people have sat comfortably in the pews. But now they may be indignant. This minister
of theirs has plans for larger work? He wants to be set free financially
to carry them out? Well then, let him pay his bribe: not a bribe in
money, for *they* have that, but the subtler bribe of silence about
matters they do not want to hear discussed. Let him be subservient
to their authority. Then they will see that he gets a reward. By their
support, they will assure him of what appear to be more ample
facilities for preaching the gospel—provided it be what they call "the
pure gospel," uncontaminated by relevance to controversial issues
of actual life. Otherwise, they will do their best to keep him shut up,
as Felix "left Paul bound."

IV

The final and most important fact about Felix is what may have been
happening in his conscience. Underneath his hard surface there was
something vulnerable. That is true of almost every man, even of the
man whose over-all record seems conspicuously bad. The sense of
moral accountability may be covered up, but it is not easily got
rid of altogether. When Paul spoke about "justice and self-control
and future judgment," no emotion may have shown on Felix's face,
but there was uneasiness inside him. With half of himself he could be
contemptuous of the moral challenge which this man before him
sounded, but he could not stop the reverberations set up in the half of
his soul that was still sensitive. "Judgment to come": he could affect
to be cynical about that, but not altogether cynical. He knew enough
about life to understand that there are such things as cause and consequence; and that though the mills of the gods grind slowly, they
may grind exceeding small. So he may have had his moment when he

looked at his record and saw the evil in it, and was almost moved to turn to this Paul who spoke with such authority of conviction, and see whether Paul could somehow help him get rid of his disquiet.

There may be the crucial instant when the destiny of a man's spirit trembles in the balance. "Yes, I will talk with this Paul, and learn what he might have to say to me," was the decision which Felix almost made. But what he actually said to Paul was this: "Go away for the present; when I have an opportunity"—or as the King James Version translates the words, *when I have a convenient season*—"I will summon you."

But the "convenient season" for the kind of talk with Paul which might have been spiritually transforming never came—as tragically also for other men the transforming experience which waits for a convenient season may never come. The ultimate realities of life cannot be casually laid hold on. They cannot be made the playthings of convenience. *"Now* is the acceptable time; behold, now is the day of salvation." The story of Felix ends with one curt statement. Porcius Festus arrived to be governor in his place. Felix had been summarily removed, because of accusations made to Rome against him. So his record ends in emptiness. His life, which might have had some great meaning if he had responded to the gospel which was preached before him, had none. He merely disappears into the dark.

16.

Real Greatness

I was not disobedient to the heavenly vision.

ACTS 26:19

WHEN PAUL, the Apostle, near the end of his career stood before Felix, the Roman, and spoke "upon faith in Christ Jesus," Felix had his chance to learn what might have made him a different man. But his pride and the cynical self-assurance which life had bred in him made him unable to believe it. It seemed beneath his own importance to admit that this Paul had anything that was crucial to say to him, the man of prestige and of power. He could not see the greatness that is of the spirit. And often in every generation that greatness is not seen or understood; neither the fact of it, nor what it is.

Not long after Felix had gone his way into oblivion, Paul was examined by two others, who according to their world's assumption had authority to judge him: Porcius Festus, who had succeeded Felix as the Roman governor, and Herod Agrippa II, who though he was only a puppet of Rome had the title of king over regions adjacent to the Lake of Galilee. Following their invitation to explain himself, Paul expanded what he had begun to say to Felix on "faith in Christ Jesus." And the first and most arresting thing he did was to tell of a vision which had come to him on the road to Damascus, and to set forth the central meaning of his life in one burning phrase, "Wherefore, O King Agrippa, I was not disobedient to the heavenly vision."

It is doubtful if those words meant anything much to Festus or to Agrippa. They were men of the world, both of them, with the worldly man's incredulity for anything out of his ken. Their eyes were on the main chance, and aside from that not much else would seem to them to matter. What did they think, then, when they heard Paul

speak of a "heavenly vision"? In imagination we may well see the
lifted eyebrows as they looked at one another. So this was the sort
of person they were called upon to try, a mad fellow, a fanatic who
followed delusions. The record in the Book of Acts informs us that,
when Paul had finished, Herod Agrippa said, in a patronizing
superiority which was half a sneer, "In a short time you think to
make me a Christian!"

Nevertheless, the significant fact is that the man who stood there
lonely and seemingly unimportant that day is the man who has
survived. Who cares anything today about Festus? Who cares anything about Agrippa? Their names are nothing but echoes from the
dead. But Paul? Has the world forgotten him? Does he not still
walk the earth as an influence more widely potent than in his lifetime
nineteen hundred years ago? The city of London is as old as Christian
history, while the life forces of one of the world's great empires flow
through its streets today; and in the center of London, towering over
every other landmark, is the dome of the great Cathedral of St. Paul.
Innumerable other churches in all lands, as we well know, carry that
same name. The thought of Paul, the spirit of Paul, the example of
Paul, have affected more multitudes of people than anyone can ever
count. One thing is certain, then; that Festus and Herod Agrippa,
who imagined that day that they were hardheaded realists, were
only the dupes of their own dull souls. Time had been on the side of
the man whom that day they doubtless smiled at as a fool.

I

Let us follow then the suggestion of those three words, the heavenly
vision. Think first of *the vision seen.*

The Bible is starred with the records of men who in one way or
another had their experience of a heavenly vision. Jacob in his
flight from Esau stops at Bethel, and in his dream he beholds a
ladder set up from earth to heaven with the angels of God ascending
and descending upon it; and from that time Jacob began to be a
different and a better man. Moses in the wilderness, at a critical
moment of his destiny, sees his vision of a bush that burned with fire
and was not consumed; and in his flaming consciousness of God he
goes back to Egypt to be the deliverer of his people. Isaiah the
prophet goes into the Temple at Jerusalem, and before his awestruck
eyes there seemed to shine the intolerable splendor of God himself
throned between the seraphim; and from that day forward Isaiah
began to shape the destiny of a nation. And Saul of Tarsus on the

Damascus road sees at midday his vision of Jesus in the sky, and by the power of that vision his whole life was turned round and set on the pathway of a new loyalty which henceforth he was to follow to his life's end. It is evident then that what men call a heavenly vision is not hallucination. It can be a force so real that it lays hold of a whole career and changes it. The most crucial moment in a man's destiny may be that moment in which he sees that which the ordinary eyes may never see at all.

"As yes, but that is just the difficulty," someone may answer. "There may be miraculous awareness which comes to a few highly gifted and extraordinary spirits. These so-called 'heavenly visions' do not come to everyday men. The psychologists, perhaps, may explain how they belong to some peculiarly sensitive, not to say abnormal, temperaments. But what has this consideration of heavenly visions to do with me?"

It has to do with you because the experience which is suggested in those words is nearer to our apprehension than we think. Are there not many kinds of men who, at some time or other, are guided by illuminations which may well be called heavenly when one considers how high they are above the ordinary calculations of this earth? Whenever a poem is written, what is it that has produced it? Does the poet sit down and work out some theme with coolly balanced argument? Does he devise his rhythms and his rhymes like a man doing a sum in arithmetic? Does he manufacture his own inspiration like a man striking a match to light a candle? He does not. As he broods and meditates, and perhaps at the very moment when his own thought seems most like emptiness and shadows, suddenly a great suggestion seems to dawn above him like a bursting star. When some supreme piece of architecture is created, does it come forth simply out of plodding calculations; or has there not been some instant when the architect beheld his imagined thing of beauty not as something he had invented, but as though it suddenly were given him from above? When the musician conceives a symphony, does he feel that the music is manufactured out of himself; or rather that in some hour of rapture he had heard it drift down to him like the music of the spheres? Surely all artists and all men in every line of work who have achieved some real creation have had their moments when they have felt that they had suddenly seen something which existed there in the ideal world before they ever saw it.

Yet most of us are not poets or artists or musicians. We are only everyday people immersed generally in the humdrum work of the world. Can *we* have any "heavenly vision"?

Yes, we can have heavenly visions and *do* have them every time we are enlightened by a new idea, challenged by a new purpose, laid hold upon by a new conviction which we did not deliberately seek for, which we may even flinch from, but which we know that we cannot ignore.

> Not in entire forgetfulness,
> And not in utter nakedness,
> But trailing clouds of glory, do we come,
> From God, who is our home . . .
> The Youth who daily farther from the east
> Must travel, still is Nature's priest,
> And by the vision splendid
> Is on his way attended.[1]

There is no single one of us, no matter how much he pretends to be a creature of this earth, who can deny that he has had his moments of illumination. In a strange way often we live in two worlds.

For the most part, perhaps, we move down on the dusty levels of the uninspired and the obvious. In its more drab moments life may seem to be only a very grubby business, a mere struggle for existence, a doing of dull work for necessary wages, a routine treadmill of making enough to keep alive. In those times, our relationship to people may seem as dull as the things we do. Our thoughts do not go beyond the mechanics of the monotonous job. Other people, like things, are only so many instruments with whom unemotionally we are put in gear.

That is one aspect of life. But is there any of us who honestly can say that there is not another aspect of it? There are those hours when everything somehow is set in a new perspective. We see that the old job might be done in a new and better way. We see that the old relationship can be lifted up into a new imagination. We see that these poor plodding selves of ours can have a new shining value as helpers, lovers, friends. It is as though in the midst of a gray and murky day the fog had lifted so that the blue sky shines through. We know that we are in a bigger world than formerly we had believed. The seamy side of things vanishes, and life takes on a new significance. Something higher than this earth has looked at us, and spoken to us, and said to us, "You belong to me."

Is there anything untrue to you in that? Is there anything fantastic or imaginary in it? Is there anything to which anyone cannot say,

---

[1] Wordsworth, *Ode on Intimations of Immortality.*

"Yes, my experience confesses that this is so. If this is what you mean by the heavenly vision, I think I do have glimpses of the heavenly vision too."

When his inspiration came to Paul, it carried him to far places and to widely scattered peoples whom he helped to learn the meaning of Christ. So his life expanded into greatness. But the essential witness which a life may bear does not depend upon its circumference. What Paul learned and what Paul experienced may begin at home and be expressed at home. The man in the ordinary place who is lifting up his eyes toward the best he knows will be reflecting it where he is, and people round him will be the better because of what they see in him.

II

So the vision seen was the first element in Paul's greatness, but that could not have been decisive without *the vision obeyed.*

What would Paul do with the sudden new conception of life in the service of Christ which had dawned upon him? Would he let it be only the emotion of a moment, with no practical consequences to follow? Such it might have been; but listen to the fact. "I was *not disobedient,*" he said, "to the heavenly vision."

The following of the vision is not always an easy matter. It requires patience and devotion. It calls not only for the first awareness but for a steady will.

One of the difficulties which we may face lies in the fact that we may sometimes be confused about our exact choices. When we try to follow on the right way, we hope that that way will somehow be made clear from the beginning to the end. We want a kind of moral and spiritual certainty which will always be self-evident. But life usually does not work out in this fashion. Paul himself had his moments of perplexity and almost of discouragement, as some of his letters to his churches plainly show. A man today may commit himself to the guidance of the truest and highest light he sees. He may make up his mind that in his home, in his business, and in his public life he will live to the very best of his ability as a Christian should. But again and again he will find himself uncertain as to what the Christian way through some particular situation is. There may not seem to be any positive road of right as against an equally positive road of evil. He may not be sure that the decision he makes will lead to the end he wants; and sometimes, when the facts are very baffling, the temptation may come to think that the whole idea of a heavenly vision is illusory. Nevertheless, the man who has once committed himself to the guidance of God does have at least his sense of general direction. Through every possible confusion he will be moving toward truth and courage and kindness and helpfulness. He will still be obedient to the heavenly vision, even when he cannot see precisely where it leads, but only knows that one particular road ahead rather than another seems to be compelling.

"Ah?" but someone may say, "that glosses over too easily a deeper difficulty. If we could always see the light, even although it were only sufficient to reveal a general direction, that would be satisfying enough. But the real fact is different. Sometimes the light disappears completely. The road may be full not only of turnings but of shadows too. As in the words of Palgrave's hymn

> Comes faint and far thy voice
> From vales of Galilee;
> The vision fades in ancient shades;
> How should we follow thee?

When men want to do right and do not know where the right is, what is the answer for them then?"

Well, the answer is that we must fall back upon the reserves of moral and spiritual consciousness which have been stored up in us as the result of those earlier days when we have followed the best light we had. In human souls there is something at least of that unerring instinct which makes homing pigeons find their way to the goal through the darkest night. Something in us remembers that quarter of the compass in which the light of truth shone for us when it was last seen, and toward that quarter we can keep on moving even when we cannot clearly see.

In the biography of David Livingstone there is a great passage which is significant for our thinking now. David Livingstone was not only one of the great explorers of all time, but one of the bravest and most devoted followers of Christ and helpers of his fellow men. His biographer, considering the extraordinary steadfastness of his aim, which made him get through to achievements that would have seemed to an ordinary man impossible, is pondering the explanation of Livingstone's perception of his course of duty.

But how did he get this? First, his singleness of heart, so to speak, attracted the light: "If thine eye be single, thy whole body shall be full of light." Then, he was very clear and very minute in his prayers. Further, he was most careful to scan all the providential indications that might throw light on the Divine will. And when he had been carried so far on in the line of duty, he had a strong presumption that the line would be continued, and that he would not be called to turn back. It was in front, not in rear, that he expected to find the pillar of cloud and the pillar of fire.[2]

Can we fail to see the meaning here for us? In front, and not in the rear, he expected to find the guiding light. *That* at least we can remember in every moment when we are perplexed. When we are tempted to surrender or halt in the ways upon which we have started because they have seemed to us the way of duty, we can surely believe that as we keep going forward the light again will be revealed.

III

When the heavenly vision is once seen, and then obeyed with as steady faithfulness as a man can muster, then there comes to that man a strength which he had never known he could possess, and in which he finds *the vision vindicated.* That is the way it was with Paul. Once he had seen what his life could become in the service of Christ, nothing could daunt him. "I can do all things in him who strengthens me," he said.

Every man can learn this truth, that when a great purpose grips him all obstacles shrivel. In one of the great eastern universities a few years ago there was a man who took eight years to get his Bachelor of Arts degree. The reason was that he had no money to support himself in college; and what he did was this. He worked one year in the coal mines, came to college for one year, went back to mining coal to make the money for the next year's study, and so on with that patient alternation until he graduated. It was a hard thing to get his education thus; but not too hard for him, because he was looking ahead. He wanted the training so much that any price seemed not too high to pay for it. Why he wanted it was not chiefly for his own advantage. He wanted to be equipped for leadership in the labor movement, to make conditions better for thousands of men who had been workers like himself. That great desire was his strength.

The most significant achievements of this world are those which

[2] W. Garden Blaikie *The Personal Life of David Livingstone* (New York: Fleming H. Revell n.d.; Author's Preface dated 1880), p. 132.

are carried through in spite of difficulties that would dismay the ordinary individual and seem at first impossible to the general crowd. But they become possible when some tremendous daring and commitment looks past the difficulties and goes ahead with a determination which nothing can subdue. In the dark hours of the Second World War, England and the freedom of the Western world seemed threatened with immediate disaster—disaster which then would have befallen if there had not been a mightier fact. That mightier fact was the invincible courage to hold steadfast which was expressed in the words of Winston Churchill: "We have never looked back, never flagged, never doubted, never flinched. We were sure of our duty and we have discharged it, and will discharge it, without swerving or slackening to the end."

In the life of the spirit, as in the events of the world, the blessed fact is that when one is fully bent on going forward, no matter what the resistances in his way may seem to be, he often finds that when he goes up straight to these they are not insuperable. In John Bunyan's great allegory of *Pilgrim's Progress*, the Pilgrim on his way to the Celestial City comes to the Hill Difficulty. Up this steep and forbidding slope he goes, and then in the midst of it he is appalled to see before him two lions. He is sure that he can never get past them alive, and that there is nothing for him to do but to give up the effort and go down the hill. But at that moment he hears a voice which commands him to keep on. He does keep on; and when he comes abreast of the lions he finds that they are chained, so that neither one of them can reach him if he keeps to the straight and narrow way between. Some of the threatening facts of life are like those lions. They seem to make progress past them impossible, but actually they do not. Always there is the straight road of daring which they cannot reach, the single line of choice and effort which if we follow nothing can impede.

In the end it can be manifest that obstacles not only have not lessened life, they have enlarged it. As we look at the world within us and at the world around—and this is the more so as our experience deepens—we know that it is not by getting rid of difficulties but by realizing our own soul's growth in relation to them that life is made rich. The virile races of this earth have not been bred in the tropic zones where the climate is soft and vegetation luxurious and no one has to make much effort for existence. They have been bred in the harder regions where there is ice and cold and rocky ground, where men must work to live and meet the strenuousness of nature with stamina in themselves. The seamen of the British empire, and all great seamen in the long history of the world, have not been fashioned by smooth oceans and sunny skies, but by raging seas and storms and dark and danger. The greatest explorers have been such because they did not stick to the protected places but went out in a kind of splendid joy to match themselves against the hazardous unknown. One of the bravest spirits I know has on his bookplate the silhouette of a mountain and underneath it these words: "Not to climb is not to conquer."

And beyond all that thus has been recognized there is something still more inspiring to remember, and it is this. A man's fight with obstacles may be glorious, even though to outward appearances he does not seem to win. He may be denied immediate and apparent victory, and yet win such an inner victory that its influence will be immortal. What this means is exemplified in the heroic words found in the journal of Captain Robert F. Scott, who on his return from the South Pole died with all his remaining companions in a blizzard on the Antarctic ice. He wrote: "I may not have proved a great explorer, but we have done the greatest march ever made and come very near to great success. . . . If this diary is found, it will show that we stuck by dying companions and fought the thing out well to the end. I think this will show that the spirit of pluck and power to endure has not passed out of our race."

That spirit which Scott expressed may seem beyond our ordinary range. And still more beyond our range may seem the spirit of the great Apostle who has been the center of our thinking, who gloried in what God could work through him, notwithstanding what the world could consider disaster and defeat. But there can be a kinship with them which can be shared by every man who tried to follow the heavenly vision which has come to him in his humbler sphere. He who at the end can say, like Paul, "I have fought the good fight, I have finished the race, I have kept the faith," will have given to his world some of that quality of life which made Paul great.

17.

The Man Jesus Made Over

"So you are Simon the son of John? You shall
be called Cephas" [which means Rock].
JOHN 1:42

IN ALL the chapters of this book we have been thinking of men and
women of the Bible, and of reflections of ourselves which we may
see in them. Those reflections are not always pleasant; for the Bible
is a wide mirror, and there are few aspects of ourselves which do
not stare us in the face when we consider human nature as the
Bible portrays it. Sometimes we see the kind of life which is high-
principled and strong and true, and we say, "Thank God that at
least I *want* to be like that." Then we see evasions and faithlessness
and flat failure, and we say, "God forgive me, that is the way I
too often am." And if we have been thoughtful, we have recognized
this: that we need to be laid hold upon by a power greater than
anything we possess if what we are is to be changed into something
better. No mere personal good resolves, no satisfied "ethical culture," will save us. We must become aware of a divine love which,
in the beautiful truth of George Matheson's hymn, "followeth all
our way," and will not let us go.

What that means is embodied in the story of the man who became the best known of Jesus' first disciples. One day this man,
who had come down from Galilee to the Jordan River where John
the Baptist was preaching, came face to face with Jesus. Jesus
looked at him, and in two brief sentences he expressed the difference
between what a man is and what God can make of him. "So you
are Simon, the son of John?" he said. That now. But this man
should become more than his name up to that time had represented.
Henceforth he should be Cephas, or Peter—"which means Rock."
On the one hand, "you are . . ." On the other hand, "you shall

be . . ." In that contrast is the infinite distance over which what may have seemed the ordinary human possibility can be lifted to its fulfillment in the purposes of God.

I

Consider, to begin with, the sort of person this man was when Jesus saw him first—this man whom we always think of now as the Apostle Peter. He is not described when he first appears; but we have the advantage of seeing him in the light of our knowledge of what is told about him later in the Gospels and in the Book of Acts. From that growing picture we get an understanding of how he instinctively thought and acted, and therefore can infer how he regarded himself that day when Jesus said, "So you are Simon, the son of John?"

"Yes sir, you are right, I am Simon, son of John," he replied.

That name, to be sure, did not suggest particular distinction; yet it may be that when Simon identified himself he did so with some satisfaction. The story of his life with which we are familiar makes plain that he was a virile man who had a natural gift for leadership. In all the lists of Jesus' followers which would presently appear his name always stands first. In any group of men his presence would be felt. There was nothing pale or colorless about him. He was impetuous and outspoken, saying what he thought and felt as soon as anything occurred to him, sometimes blurting it out. And he was a man of some substance in his community. He was not anybody's hired hand. He and his brother operated their boat in the fishing fleet on the Lake of Galilee. He had a house in Capernaum where his wife and his mother-in-law lived with him. He did not say so, but it is possible that he thought Jesus might have reason to be pleased to have him for a friend.

And there *were* reasons. He had a warm heart, and all his instincts were on the side of what was right. If he gave his loyalty to anyone, he would want to go all out to make that loyalty good. "He would want to." That was his strength. But there was another side of him where weakness lay. What he wanted to do was not an assurance of what he would do. His emotions would lead in the right direction, but did he have the steadiness to keep on going that way if the road should be beset by appalling things he had not foreseen?

We learn the answer to that when we read the record of what happened later.

One day after Simon had become a follower of Jesus and he

and the other disciples were gathered about their Master at Caesarea Philippi, Jesus asked them what the people were saying about him. Who did they think he was? They told him the ideas and specula- tions that were being spread in the excited crowds: one of the prophets, Elijah come back to earth, John the Baptist risen from the dead. "But who do you say that I am?" Jesus asked. Then the devotion which by now he had begun to feel toward Jesus blazed up like a fire in Simon Peter to give a sudden illumination to his thinking, and he burst out with the tremendous word, "You are the Christ!"

It was wonderful to be in the fellowship of the Messiah. Who would not want that? But then Jesus followed Simon Peter's con- fession with an interpretation of Messiahship that seemed incredible. It would not be a triumph as men think of triumph. He said that he would have to "suffer many things, and be rejected by the elders and the chief priests and the scribes, and be killed." *That* was what he was going to face as he went up to Jerusalem.

Peter was shocked. He began to argue that Jesus could not really mean what he seemed to say. A shadow had come across the sun.

What might have begun to happen in Peter's spirit was sym- bolized perhaps by what is told of in the Gospel of Matthew as having occurred one night on the Lake of Galilee. When the disciples were in a boat, without Jesus, and a sudden violent storm dropped down across the hills and their oars could make no headway against the wind-swept water, they were terrified. Then they thought they saw Jesus coming toward them. Peter, according to the account in Matthew, cried out, "Lord, if it is you, bid me come to you on the water"; and the Lord said, "Come." But when Peter got out of the boat and tried to go to Jesus, his faith failed and he began to sink.

The two sides of his nature were in the balances, and it was not clear yet which side would prevail. There was no doubt as to which side he wanted to prevail. If he had his qualms of fear and began to be uncertain about himself, he tried to cover up that uncertainty. The Gospel of Mark says that when Jesus finally set his face to go up to Jerusalem, "those who followed were afraid." Peter was among those who followed, and he may have been afraid too. But he was not letting himself show it, and he was going ahead, all the same.

Yet the tremors which sometimes were within him had their evi- dence in the way that at critical moments he tried to talk them down. He would proclaim to others—and in that process be trying underneath to convince himself—that there was no weakness in him. Perhaps he could manage boldness by the tonic of bold words. Therefore when Jesus had gathered the whole company of the disciples round him for the Last Supper in the Upper Room and warned them that in the dangers ahead they might desert him and be scattered like sheep, Peter declared, "Though they all fall away, I will never fall away"; and when Jesus told him that he would, he protested all the more vehemently, "Even if I must die with you, I will not deny you."

That is what he wanted to be true, but there had not been built up in him yet the strength that would make it true.

From the Upper Room Jesus led the disciples out to the Garden of Gethsemane. There, with a sudden blaze of torches, the armed guard from the high priest came to seize him. Peter had a sword and he struck out with it once. But when Jesus stopped him, it did not seem as though there was anything else that he could do. The Gospel of Matthew records that when Jesus had been seized, "then all the disciples forsook him and fled."

If that desolate statement expressed the fact concerning the other disciples, perhaps it was not quite the fact concerning Peter. He may have been caught in the first near-panic of escape from Gethsemane, but he did not quite run off and hide. When Jesus was taken by the guard to the house of Caiaphas the high priest, Peter followed, and he got into the courtyard. In spite of everything, he wanted to keep as close to Jesus as he could. Hadn't he said, "Even if I must die with you, I will never deny you"?

But now *that* would happen! He who had asserted his loyalty so loudly, would deny his Lord. The last of his self-confidence would be broken, the last of his imagined integrity destroyed.

Here is the way the account in one of the Gospels runs:

And as Peter was below in the courtyard, one of the maids of the High Priest came; and seeing Peter warming himself, she looked at him, and said, "You also were with the Nazarene, Jesus." But he denied it, saying, "I neither know nor understand what you mean." And he went out into the gateway. And the maid saw him, and began again to say to the bystanders, "This man is one of them." But again he denied it. And after a little while again the bystanders said to Peter, "Certainly you are one of them; for you are a Galilean." But he began to invoke a curse on himself and to swear, "I do not know this man of whom you speak." And immediately the cock crowed a second time. And Peter remembered how Jesus had said to him, "Before the cock crows twice, you will deny me three times." And he broke down and wept.

No wonder!

It seemed the end of everything for Simon Peter. He was back to being only Simon now, and a Simon exposed as not even the man he thought he was, but only a hollow shell. That day when Jesus had first spoken his name he had been a man well regarded by those who knew him. He had self-respect; some pride, even in himself. It did not occur to him that he could be an ignominious failure. That perhaps had been the trouble. He had not looked deep into his own nature and seen the weakness that was covered up by what he thought was his self-sufficiency. And now he knew the shattering truth.

Are there not some in every time who have had that bitter revelation? Is there not some echo of it in us? Who is there that must not confess to aspects in our lives which fill us with shame?— expectations to which we did not measure up, tests at which we flinched because of some sudden cowardice, failures in friendship when someone looked to us for steady loyalty and we let him down. If facts like those are burned in our remembrance, then we know—or ought to know—why Simon Peter "broke down and wept."

II

What now could save him? Nothing that he could do. Only the remembrance of what his Master had done for him, and the promise from that same Master that would not fail.

For Jesus had said to him, "You are Simon"; but he had also said, "You shall be called Peter, which means Rock."

Two great certainties from those words came to Simon Peter in the hour of his humiliation. The first was that Jesus had known him better than he knew himself. Those clairvoyant eyes had looked all through him and seen him as he was: seen the limitations which he, Simon, did not like to recognize, seen the dark corners in his soul, and yet had taken him as a disciple. If he had thought deeply enough about that, he would have known that there was no use in his trying to put up a front—as he *had* tried to put a front in the Upper Room when he told everybody how dependable he would be. Jesus had perceived the real fact then, had said to him. "Satan has desired to sift you as wheat." Well, Satan had sifted him now, and it looked as though all that Satan had found was chaff. Was this then all that Jesus had seen that day when he said, "So you are Simon?"

No, it was not all. It could not have been all. For here was the saving wonder: Jesus, seeing him as he was, had nevertheless accepted him. Jesus, seeing his deficiencies, had seen something else; seen the possibilities in him that could be developed. Jesus had said, "You shall be called Rock." God knows he had not shown any sign of being a Rock yet. But Jesus had said he would be; and though he had failed, the promise of Jesus would not, could not fail. In the hour of his deepest shame, stripped now of all his pride and would-be self-sufficiency, he held on to that. Jesus would not let him go. Here was the one thing that kept him from going out and hanging himself, as Judas did.

Then the spiritual miracle was on the verge of being brought to its fulfillment. Simon Peter, the man who had denied his Master was about to become the man made over. There were to be days of agony first. He was to see Jesus crucified, and know that he could never go to him now and pour out the passion of his soul's repentance. But even in what might have been his utmost hopelessness there came to him a remembrance of the love of Jesus so great that in it even he could be forgiven. And being forgiven, he must go forward now to justify what his Lord had said he must become.

So we try to think of, and to put into words, what went on in Peter's mind and heart. But beyond all thoughts and words of ours—unless we in some measure have experienced it—is the ineffable fact expressed in what the New Testament has handed down as The First Letter of Peter, in which it is written, "Blessed be the God and Father of our Lord Jesus Christ! By his great mercy we have been born anew to a living hope through the resurrection of Jesus Christ from the dead." To Peter, and to Peter first, according to the tradition of the early Church, Jesus alive again after his crucifixion, Jesus victorious over sin and death, was made manifest. By the fire of that experience, tremendous as the volcanic fires that formed the mountains of the earth, Peter was recreated as the Rock.

We can see the new man as he appears in the Book of Acts.

One day he was going up, with John, to the Temple in Jerusalem. At the gate of the Temple a lame man was sitting, and he begged the two of them for alms. It was Peter who answered: "I have no silver and gold, but I give you what I have." And what was it that now he did have? Power: the power of a new faith, not in himself but in the mercy of God which he had seen in Jesus. "In the name of Jesus Christ of Nazareth, walk!" he said to the lame man; and at that command the lame man did stand up, and went into the Temple "walking and leaping and praising God."

When a crowd gathered, astonished at what had happened, Peter began to preach to them of Jesus—of Jesus whom he had denied a little while before in Caiaphas' court. He and John were promptly arrested, and the next day brought before the high priest and the rest of the ruling Council. They faced now the same men who had tried their Master and had crucified him. But now in both of them, and especially in Peter, the transformation had been wrought. They had a boldness which astonished their examiners. They would not be silenced. They would go on proclaiming to Jew and to Roman alike the gospel of their crucified but risen Lord; and that is what Peter did.

It was Peter who answered the plea that came from the centurion, Cornelius; went to his house and baptized him as the first convert from the Gentile world. It was Peter who stood up in the Council of the church in Jerusalem and defended the missionary evangelism of Paul and Barnabas who had loosed the gospel altogether from Jewish limitations. "The grace of the Lord Jesus," he said, could reach out to all men—just as it had reached out redeemingly to him.

After the Council in Jerusalem at which he spoke, there is no further explicit record of Peter in the Book of Acts. But through all the traditions which have come down from the early Church his looming figure moves: as going at length to Rome; meeting there John Mark who, helped by Peter's memories, would be the writer of the first Gospel; caught in Nero's persecution, and put on trial for his life. In Lloyd C. Douglas' *The Big Fisherman*, there is a description so expressive of the essential fact that it deserves to be remembered. Peter is arraigned before Fabius, the Roman judge, because the Christians had been accused of treason to the empire.

"Is it true, then," the Judge had demanded, "that you believe in the coming of a King who will rule the world?"

"Yes," Peter had replied boldly, "that is true!" . . .

"And what becomes of Caesar?" demanded the Judge, sternly.

"Our Christus, sir," declared Peter, "will rule the world, and every knee shall bow before him."

The heavy silence now had been broken only by the rattling of the papyrus sheet as the judge recorded his decision on the indictment. Then he arose and said:

"You have left this court no alternative, Peter. The law is the law. It is not in our province to amend it, not even to save the life of a misguided fanatic. You will be taken hence to prison and in thirty days you will be put to death!"

The next day one of his friends came to see him.

"Peter," he began, gently reproachful, "why did you do it? Fabius was doing his best to save you. . . . Did you have to say that the Master's Kingdom would rule the world?"
   "I had to tell the truth," Peter replied. "I disowned my Master once. I think he depends on me not to do it again."[1]

So Peter died a martyr's death, and in his dying bore witness to the power which had come to him. Everyone knows how the Roman Catholic Church has magnified the authority he is alleged to have had and to have transmitted to the popes of Rome. Some of that elaborate doctrine of Peter's supremacy is only pious fiction. But underneath all the elaboration, and the one thing that could have made it possible, must have been this fact: that the man who once was the undependable Simon *had* become the man made over, who could be looked upon as Rock.

III

What happened to Peter was a long time ago, but the spiritual reality of it can be repeated in every time. The Master whom he had loved and who loved him was not dead. His body had been crucified; but he himself, risen from a tomb that could not hold him, was and is alive and bringing life—let loose in the world where neither death nor time can destroy him, where no evil in men's hearts can over-come him, where no change of circumstance can hide his resurgent power! He can be the Lord and Savior to lift us, as he lifted Simon Peter, out of humiliation into hope that, in spite of everything, we may yet be made into the sort of persons that the grace of God would have us be.

"Made into the sort of persons that the grace of God would have us be." Those are not words only. They are the promise of the living fact which can be accomplished for every would-be Christian who opens mind and heart to the everlasting influence of Jesus. Dick Sheppard, Vicar of Saint-Martin-in-the-Fields, at the heart of London, known and beloved as few men in any generation have been known and loved, wrote this which was true of himself and which he

[1] Lloyd C. Douglas, *The Big Fisherman* (Boston: Houghton Mifflin Co., 1948), pp. 575–576.

helped multitudes to understand: "The secret of a life that can be used of God will be sensitiveness to Jesus Christ. An attempted intimacy with Him must precede every other consideration. He will be the centre—all else the circumference. . . . With Him there can come that massive faith in God and His goodness upon which Jesus' whole life and death were staked. . . . Jesus will become to us not the conclusion of an argument or a dogma or a legend, but a living abiding Personality nearer than the hands or feet."[2] When Dick Sheppard wrote that, he was expressing what he had learned by living it—living what Archbishop Lang had said to him at the beginning of his ministry: "Let yourself go. Let yourself go in a simple, sustained trustful surrender of yourself to the great Captain and offer all your services. . . . Let the thought of the great Love which has chosen you, called you, enter into you. Open yourself out to it as the arid sand lies open to the inflowing tide. Realize all it means to be thus chosen by the Infinite Love to go out and witness to it and fight for it, and let all your manhood welcome it and give yourself over to it."[3]

And if we ask *how* the spirit of Jesus can become redeeming, here is at least part of the answer concerning that reality which many have experienced, beyond what any can finally express.

He becomes redeeming—though this may seem a strange word to begin with—by his relentlessness. Simon Peter once when he felt himself confronted by the majesty of Jesus, cried out, "Depart from me, for I am a sinful man, O Lord." Or in simpler English, "Please let me alone, Lord! I cannot bear what you expect of me." But deep down he did not want to be let alone, and he knew that Jesus would not let him go. So it is with us—even though there are moments when we think we would like to have him go away and stop confronting us. These stirrings of our conscience, this stripping away of our compromises and excuses when we hear his voice, this troubling compulsion to do better when it would be so much easier to stay as we are: how much sometimes we might wish to be quit of that disturbance! But we cannot escape him. Like the Hound of Heaven, he follows us with

> Unhurrying chase
> And unperturbed pace
> Deliberate speed, majestic instancy.

[2] H. R. L. Sheppard, *The Human Parson* (London: John Murray, 1924), pp. 25, 27.

[3] R. Ellis Roberts, *H. R. L. Sheppard, Life and Letters* (London: John Murray, 1942), p. 47.

Meanwhile, the reason why in our inmost selves we do not want to escape this relentless pursuit is because we know that what Francis Thompson called *The Hound of Heaven* is actually the heart of heaven. It is love that follows us and will not let us stay unsought. In the *Washington Post* in January, 1965, there was an account of a young American—Donald Dawson by name—whose brother was a lieutenant in the military forces in Vietnam and had disappeared, presumably captured by the Viet Cong. The brother from home had gone to Vietnam and set out at the peril of his own life along the jungle trails, having broadcast to the guerrillas a promise of everything he had as reward if his brother were recovered. When asked what kept him going in what might have seemed so hopeless a search he answered, "I must find him. That's what I came out here for." In those words he symbolized as far as our little approximation can, the ministry of Jesus. He came to seek the lost. He came to say concerning the least of us, to say concerning you and me, "*I must find him.*"

If the man who had disappeared in Vietnam should be found, certainly he could have henceforth a new sense of the value he had in the eyes of the one who had come to save him. Something must happen in his estimate of his own life because of the devotion which had reached out to rescue it. He could not well be content to be a mean or small person after what had been sacrificed for him. That is the way it was with those whom Jesus sought, and that is the way it can be now. The men and women whom Jesus reclaimed— Simon, the undependable who was destined to be Peter the Rock, Matthew who until Jesus called him was content to be nothing more than a tax-gatherer, Mary Magdalene in her wayward passion— would never have known who they really were until his love made them know the possibilities in themselves which he had seen. That is what he will do for you. He will cause you to see yourself in a new dimension. You cannot settle down to be only what you were. He will show you, as he showed Simon Peter, the sins you need to be saved from; he will make you feel the strength of the love you are saved by, and he will help you trust the life redeemed which you can be saved into.

18.

Life Fulfilled

Christ in you, the hope of glory.
COLOSSIANS 1:27

"SEE YOURSELF in the Bible." That has been the purpose running through the chapters of this book, and what may have been the result?

First, perhaps, a more specific realization of what we are. Somewhere among the figures of the Bible we see our own inner qualities objectified. "Yes, sometimes I am like that," we say. Sometimes like Esau in his casual unconcern for the values that go beyond the immediate moment. Sometimes like David in the hot urging of the flesh, or like Ahab in his cold unconcern for whatever stood in the path of his own advantage. Sometimes like the bridesmaids in the parable of the wedding feast, who let their lights go out and came so late that for them the door was shut. Sometimes like Peter, full of good intentions but undependable when the chips were down. "So it is," we may acknowledge. "I recognize more about myself than I recognized before."

But if that were all, it would be a sorry end. We can be glad if the Bible is a truthful mirror, but we want something more than that: more than seeing ourselves reflected in those so human and imperfect figures of whom the Bible is full. We want to find there a power by which we can be changed. Who and what is there in the Bible that is *not* just like ourselves, but of a divine difference which can take hold of us and make us other than we now are?

The answer is in the One to whom all the rest of the Bible leads up. Plenty of figures in the Bible are the mirrors in which we see our limitations; but then came Jesus, who had in himself, and brought to those he touched, a life that was fed by a power which has no limits. Therefore, as the climax of our thinking, we want to consider as surely as we can just what it was that Jesus did for his disciples, and what his spirit can do for any of us who look to him now.

I

The first thing he gave was his companionship: the warm, living fact of that. Imagination leaps at the thought of what it meant to the four fishermen on the Lake of Galilee that day when the man of Nazareth stood on the strand as they were bringing their boats in and said to them, "Come with me!" and they did go with him, to be close to him, to share with him the little things of every day, to know him just as the friend they loved, before they knew the full wonder of what he incomparably was. They went with him to a wedding feast, like that at Cana. They saw him stop to watch the children playing in the market place, and take up into his arms the little ones the mothers brought to him. They watched him go with equal naturalness to the house of Simon the Pharisee, or to sit down somewhere else "with publicans and sinners," to the Pharisee's shocked surprise. To be with him made all life open out into something wider and warmer than it could have been before. Dorothy Sayers, in *The Man Born to Be King* has made all the fact of it vivid as she imagines what Matthew, the tax-gatherer might have said as he described what happened on the day when Jesus called him from his unsavory business to be a disciple.

I looked up—and there he was. . . . I stared at him, and he stared at me. . . . I started shuffling my feet. And he smiled. You know the way he smiles sometimes all of sudden—and he says, "Follow me." I couldn't believe my ears. I tumbled out of my desk, and away he went up the street, and I went after him. I could hear people laughing—and somebody spat at me—but I didn't seem to care." [And when he was asked] "What happened to all your belongings?" [he answered,] "I never gave 'em a thought—not for a week. Then my brother hunted me up and asked me what I thought I was doing. "Sell the whole lot up," I said, "or do what you like, I've done with it. And I'm having a wonderful time."[1]

That is how men felt when they were in the human companionship of Jesus. They knew that no part of ordinary life was alien to him. He could enter into all of it, and take them with him; and they knew that in whatever *they* had to do, he would be there with them.

[1] (London: Victor Gollancz Ltd., 1943), p. 121.

"Well, that was the fact long ago," we might acknowledge. "It is all a beautiful memory, brightening the record of the days when Jesus walked in Galilee and Judaea. But he was crucified, and that must have been the end of anything that could be called companionship with him."

But the fact was different; and here we come into touch with the everlasting dynamic of Christian experience. For the minds and hearts of the men who had loved him, Jesus crucified was not dead. His living spirit came back to them, to illumine their thinking, to shape their purposes, to turn their weakness into strength. It was so with Peter and John, about whom the threatening authorities were astonished when they saw these men's "boldness," and "recognized that they had been with Jesus." It was so with Stephen who in his martyrdom turned upon those who killed him a face "like the face of an angel." It was so with Paul, who being lifted up to his tremendous daring and endurance by a power beyond his own could say, "It is no longer I who live, but Christ who lives in me." And when Charles Kingsley, one of the great Christians of the nineteenth century, was asked what was the source of his strength, he answered, "I have a Friend."

The influence upon us of one whose actual face we cannot see and whose voice we cannot hear is not something strange or unfamiliar. A boy or man is away from home—drafted into the army, for instance, in a time of war. There is danger in the front lines; there is danger too when he gets out of them for a while into the back area. Up front, the tension might make a coward of him; out of the lines, he may try to forget all that he is afraid of by getting drunk. He is cut off from everything he has depended on, and he is so lonely that nothing seems to matter much. Then he gets a letter from home: a letter full of the steady pride his father and mother have in him, or the devotion of the girl he loves. From that moment he is not alone. A spiritual presence is with him that will not let him go—and a trust which he knows he must not let down.

That is the way it is with the comradeship of Christ. Because the love of God was, and is, in Jesus, his spirit breaks through every obstacle of time and circumstance; and comes most surely to those who have most need. Men know that there is nothing they can experience which he does not understand; for he faced homelessness and having "nowhere to lay his head"; he knew what it meant to be rejected by those who ought to have been loyal to him; he met ignorance and wickedness and what seemed disaster, and yet triumphed over them all. In that intensely moving book, *Through the Valley of the Kwai,*[2] Captain Ernest Gordon of the British army, captured by the Japanese in the Second World War, has described what happened in the prison camp where he and others suffered horrors which made men almost surrender to complete degradation and despair. All the religion *he* had were a few leftover ideas from Sunday school. But there came to him one day an Australian sergeant "who had something on his mind, but it took him a little time before he could bring himself to speak of it. Finally he said, . . . 'We're fed up with all we see around here. . . . No sir, it ain't good anyway you look at it. It's rotten, rotten, rotten. . . . My cobbers and I have given this a lot of thought. We've all seen the worst there is—right? Now we feel there must be something better—somewhere. So we want to have another go at this Christianity." And would he as an officer help them to think it out?

Then—"Through our readings and our discussions we came to know Jesus. He was one of us. He would understand our problems because they were the sort of problems he had faced himself. Like us, he often had no place to lay his head, no food . . . , no friends in high places. . . . He too had known the suffering, rejection and disappointments that are part of the fabric of life. As we read and talked, he became flesh and blood. . . . He was a man we could understand and admire . . . a leader we could follow. . . . the Crucifixion told us that God was in our midst, suffering with us. . . . We stopped complaining about our own. Faith would not save us from it, but it would take us through it."

And it did. The spiritual miracle was that the spirit of Jesus got into the camp, putting an end to men "kicking their mates in the teeth when they're down, stealing from each other and from the dead ones," organizing everybody instead to help each other. "There was a general reawakening. Men began to smile—even to laugh—and to sing." So that one night Captain Gordon could say, "They were singing 'Jerusalem the Golden.' . . . The words of the grand old hymn seemed symbolic to me. Maybe Jerusalem, the Kingdom of God, is here after all, 'with milk and honey blest.' Maybe man 'shall not live by bread alone' (or 'rice alone,' as we were literally doing). Maybe there is milk and honey of the spirit that puts hope into a man's eyes and a song on his lips."

That was what happened for the prison camp when Jesus as a companion had become real to men who needed an infinite Friend and the spirit of Jesus had been let loose in their world.

[2] (New York: Harper & Row, 1962), pp. 115, 116, 137, 139, 145.

II

Yet it is true that the coming-near of Jesus may have another aspect. It is written in the Gospel of Matthew that the angel who foretold the birth of Jesus said of him, "He will save his people from their sins"; and all of us whose consciences are alive know that we do have sins we need to be saved from. But the awareness of those sins and the thought of Jesus in relationship to them may at first be dismaying. There was a day—as we have remembered—when Simon Peter felt that he could not bear to be where Jesus was and to stand in the scrutiny of his eyes. "Please go away, Lord" was his instinctive cry. And when Mary Magdalene came into the house of Simon the Pharisee where Jesus was at dinner, she felt herself unfit to look into his face; and what she did was to kneel beside him, while her tears fell upon his feet.

In his presence, men and women condemned themselves, because they saw how far away they were from the beauty of life that was in him. They faced then an inevitable self-judgment; and so do we. And this self-judgment in relation to what was revealed in Jesus may come to us when we may not be consciously thinking of Jesus at all, but when we are confronted nevertheless by the reality of him as it is shown forth in some man or woman whose spirit reflects him. We may be going along quite complacently, satisfied with ourselves, until something in that other person opens our eyes to a fullness of existence to which we had been blind. We had thought that we were as good as we needed to be; or rather, we had not thought about the matter at all, but merely taken ourselves for granted since we had not seen any better revelation which could shock us by its contrast. Then one day we suddenly became aware of that other life and of its difference from us. We see this man at our side quietly rise in an emergency to a level of moral courage which takes our breath away. We see him make a choice which shows that his decisive loyalty has been transferred long ago from the common plane of his own interests up to that point which is commanded by honor and truth and God. We see him taking upon his shoulders unselfish burdens, and helping those in our human pilgrimage who stumble when they come to the hard hills. We see his figure outlined against the sky, while we are down in the valleys cultivating the easy fields of our own interests. Then—perhaps for the first time—we begin to see ourselves as we really are. We are ashamed of our complacency. We grow restless in the kind of common living with which yesterday we were content. We know that we have sinned against the real meaning of life which, now that we have seen it, we know we cannot any more deny.

The important point for many of us is that when we stand in the presence of anything that is like Jesus it is not only our overt sins which seem condemned. We may not have been guilty of any very glaring wickedness. We might think that morally we are as respectacle as the average person. But what do we amount to in comparison with him who "came not to be served, but to serve"? Those who say the General Confession in the Book of Common Prayer are rightly led to acknowledge not only that "we have done those things which we ought not to have done," but also that "we have left undone those things which we ought to have done." It is the latter fact which may be the most grievous burden upon our conscience. Our shame is in the fact of emptiness where the record of something fine and lovely might have been. There comes upon us like a shadow the memory of the times—the too many times!—when we have been stupid and indifferent; when in our hard preoccupation with our own concerns we did not even see the need of someone precious to us for an understanding that we did not show; and when we missed the chance for the kindness and compassion which we might have brought to someone whose heart was sore:

> The ill-timed truth we might have kept—
> Who knows how sharp it pierced and stung!
> The word we had not sense to say—
> Who knows how grandly it had rung?[3]

To realize these aspects of ourselves is certainly not calculated to make us proud and glad. On the contrary, we could be driven instead to go and pour dust upon our heads in humiliation for all the blunders we have committed and all the beauty to which we have been blind.

Does it seem then that we have moved into a contradiction? We began by thinking of the beautiful possible fact of the companionship of Jesus. But then we remembered that when he is made real to us the immediate result may be condemnation. How can that be "good news"?

Because the condemnation we feel is not *his* condemnation, but ours. In the light that shines from him we do condemn ourselves. And that is good. If we are to be saved from our sins we must feel

[3] Edward Rowland Sill, *The Fool's Prayer.*

them acutely enough to *want* to be saved, and to want the One who can save us. That is exactly what happened with the first disciples. Looking at Jesus they saw their own unworthiness, but also they saw in him the love of God which would take what little goodness they had and make it grow. Slumbering aspirations in them began to stir. This Master whom they had begun to follow, this confident Jesus, believed in them. He thought of them not as the ordinary and humdrum characters they had always been. He thought of them as children of God, meant to attain fulfillment. So they began to move in the direction of Jesus' belief—Simon Peter, James, John, Andrew, Mary, Martha, and all the rest; began to see their faces in the majestic mirror of Jesus' expectation. The vast suggestion of his belief was continually at work in them. With his help they would not fail him. If not today, at least sometime they might measure up to what he expected of them.

No words in the New Testament have been held more precious or recited oftener than these from the Gospel of John: "God so loved the world that he gave his only Son, that whoever believes in him should not perish, but have eternal life. For God sent the Son into the world, not to condemn the world, but that the world might be saved through him." Because of Jesus whose redeeming purpose took him all the way to Gethsemane and the cross, men have dared to believe that what the Gospel says is true: and that if God loves the world, it must mean that the human souls in it—including ours— have in them a divine spark which God put there and which he means to save. That is a conviction which has been needed in every generation, and is acutely needed now. In much of our modern literature, and in some of the popular magazines, there is a contrary idea that rises from a spring of sour cynicism and flows like a stream of dirty water over areas of life where the gardens of the spirit ought to grow. There is a cult of depreciation, and many who think themselves in the mode of present-day smartness accept its withering spread. Too many voices, some of them malevolent and some just tired and disillusioned, are suggesting that existence is only a tawdry farce. There is no such thing as love, but only lust disguised; no such thing as unselfishness, but only crafty instincts seeking covertly to achieve their ends; no such thing as high-hearted devotion and clean happiness but only sex license and the sniggering cackle of dirty jokes; no such thing as a human being with the light of God's purpose in his eyes but only a poor biological puppet, following his unlovely behavioristic urge. That is what we are bidden to listen to and believe by some of our so-called modern prophets.

But against that backstairs whispering the truth that great souls have known is like a trumpet sounded before the opening gates of a wider world. It is the note of faith in spite of all our faults, and a trust in a love that means not to condemn but to save. Lay hold then upon the heavenly possibilities, and be bold to say: "I believe in Jesus Christ. I believe in the redemption that he came to bring. I believe in the reality of his belief in men. I trust in the power of his belief in what he can wake in me!"

Sometimes in our human relationships we can catch at least a partial reflection of what the infinite love may be, and how it waits for us before we know that it is there. In a magazine years ago there appeared "A Letter from a Mother to Her Son," in which she dwelt upon the memories they shared: memories which were beautiful and glad, and yet, like all reflections of our human limitations, were sometimes wistful too. In the final paragraph she wrote:

By and by the wisdom and the love and the beauty will not bewilder and paralyze and choke us, filling us with shame and humiliation as they do now. It is really foolish and a bit high-handed to fuss overmuch about our helplessness. Our mistakes must have been expected and inevitable. The hand that reaches out to help us must be quite sure we won't grasp it the first or even the hundredth time; but when we get ready and see the need of it, the hand is there, strong and kind, with no impatience that we were so long.[4]

So the hand of God which was revealed in the love of Jesus does reach out to us again and again, although we are so slow to grasp it; reaches out in mercy and forgiveness for the failures of yesterday, and with encouragement for the days that yet may be.

III

It was promised of Jesus, as we have been remembering, that he would save his people from their sins. Also he himself expressed the ultimate purpose of his coming when he said that those who look to him shall have life and have more of it than they had ever known before.

Sometimes people imagine that if the influence of Jesus becomes controlling it will mean restriction. To be saved from their sins— yes, they think they want that; but at the same time they have a sort of lingering apprehension. Maybe being a Christian means

4 *The Churchman,* December, 1937.

chiefly giving up this and that, cutting existence into a narrowed pattern, a harsh denial of pretty much everything that might be spontaneous. Will there be any satisfaction in life if it has to be a bondage? No, there wouldn't be. But the blunder is in supposing that the man who has felt the attraction of Christ is in bondage, while the one who has never felt it is free. The man left all to himself could be free to waste his possibilities, if that is what he wants; free to get trapped by the mean things that can clip the wings of his soul. But if he wants his life enlarged, then he can listen instead to the one who said, "I came that they may have life, and have it abundantly."

Jesus is not understood until we see how instinctively he entered into all happy human relationships, and brought a new glow to every group into which he came. It is written that as a boy in Nazareth he "increased in wisdom and stature, and in favor with God and man." When he looked out upon his world it was with eyes sensitive to everything that could be beautiful: to the lilies in the Galilean fields, to children playing in the market place, to birds building their nests in the hedgerows, to shepherds caring for the sheep. He was at home in the synagogue, and equally at home out on the lake shore where the hardy men of the fishing fleet came in. He went to a wedding feast in Cana, and to the dinner to which Matthew the tax-gatherer had invited his friends. When his enemies tried to discredit him, they did so by presenting a picture of him which even in its sour distortion bore witness to his eager and outgoing spirit. They said he was "a gluttonous man and a wine-bibber, a friend of publicans and sinners." Friend to all sorts of human beings he was, and most instinctively to those who needed him most, with a friendship which did not stoop or condescend, but in its clean strength made men want to come up to the level on which they saw him move.

Only a sorry blindness to the truth can make men ever think that Christianity somehow means separation from the wideness and wonder of the world, though that is a blindness which has often prevailed. Too many have supposed that it was only in some fenced-off part of existence that they could be fully serving Christ. The minister could be "a man of God"; but the mechanic, the farmer, the clerk, the cab driver and the cook, though they might be necessary parts of this world's existence, have nothing much to do with the world of the spirit. But those who have the mind of Christ know better than that. George Herbert, back in the early seventeenth century, expressed what was true then and will remain true as long as time shall last.

Teach me, my God and King
In all things thee to see:
And what I do in anything
To do it as for thee.

A servant with this cause
Makes drudgery divine,
Who sweeps a room as for thy laws,
Makes that, and the action, fine.

If the heart is set upon the highest, if the whole spirit is mastered by a desire for excellence, if some measure of Christlike devotion and unselfish love is poured into the common task, then to that man or woman will come what Jesus promised as the gift here and hereafter of the more abundant life.